
HAVE YOU BEEN

HEXED?

About the Author

Alexandra Chauran (Issaquah, WA) is a second-generation fortune-teller. As a professional psychic intuitive for over a decade, she serves thousands of clients in the Seattle area and globally through her website. She is certified in tarot, contributes to Horoscopes.com, and has been interviewed on National Public Radio and local radio stations. Visit her online at Earthshod.com.

To Write to the Author

If you wish to contact the author or would like more information about this book, please write to the author in care of Llewellyn Worldwide, and we will forward your request. Llewellyn Worldwide cannot guarantee that every letter written to the author can be answered, but all will be forwarded. Please write to:

Alexandra Chauran
⅄ Llewellyn Worldwide
2143 Wooddale Drive
Woodbury, MN 55125-2989

Please enclose a self-addressed stamped envelope for reply, or $1.00 to cover costs. If outside the USA, enclose an international postal reply coupon.

HAVE YOU BEEN HEXED?

RECOGNIZING AND BREAKING CURSES

ALEXANDRA CHAURAN

Llewellyn Publications
Woodbury, Minnesota

FIRST EDITION
First Printing, 2013

Book design by Bob Gaul
Cover art: Decorative rule lines © iStockphoto.com/piart
         Grunge frame © iStockphoto.com/Duncan Walker
         Hands © iStockphoto.com/Özgür Donmaz
Cover design by Ellen Lawson
Editing by Laura Graves
Interior art: Decorative rule lines © iStockphoto.com/piart

Llewellyn Publications is a registered trademark of Llewellyn Worldwide Ltd.

Library of Congress Cataloging-in-Publication Data (Pending)
978-0-7387-3620-4

Llewellyn Worldwide Ltd. does not participate in, endorse, or have any authority or responsibility concerning private business transactions between our authors and the public.

All mail addressed to the author is forwarded, but the publisher cannot, unless specifically instructed by the author, give out an address or phone number.

Any Internet references contained in this work are current at publication time, but the publisher cannot guarantee that a specific location will continue to be maintained. Please refer to the publisher's website for links to authors' websites and other sources.

Llewellyn Publications
A Division of Llewellyn Worldwide Ltd.
2143 Wooddale Drive
Woodbury, MN 55125-2989
www.llewellyn.com

Printed in the United States of America

Contents

Introduction

Imagine it is the worst time of your life: in the blink of an eye, everything is going wrong. Perhaps you are suddenly fired from your job for no particular reason, and on the same day your social life disappears in a puff of smoke. You come home, weary and worried about your finances, only to find that your significant other is acting like a different person, and announces that you are being left for another lover. Devastated, you are caught completely off-guard. Wasn't it only yesterday that you felt secure in your relationship and your career? Things are going so badly that you do some soul-searching, looking for something deeper that may be influencing your life.

You find yourself at the doorstep of a psychic, asking for a reading on what might be happening. She welcomes you inside tenderly, like an old friend, but seems shocked when she begins to read for you. Trembling in fear, she announces that you have a powerful hex upon you, and asks if you have any enemies. Surprised, your head spins with the possibilities. Nothing has been going right in your life…could an enemy be to blame? You have several coworkers who have been spreading lies about you, and even your best friend seems to have turned on you. Perhaps it is this very friend who has become your beloved's new lover.

The psychic nods compassionately, acting as the first listening ear you've had in a while, and then tells you that she has the solution. She asks for a sum of money larger than your last paycheck, but assures you that it will be returned to you, possibly with riches beyond your wildest dreams. She only needs the money to place upon an altar during a powerful magic spell under the full moon. This will bring back your lover, reinstate you in your job with a raise, and completely eliminate the curse. As a bonus, the spell will get back at the person who hexed you in the first place. The benefits are so tempting that you immediately wonder if you can ask your parents for the money. You tell the psychic that you will have to think about it, and her demeanor changes. Angry and fearful at the same time, she tells you that if you don't have her perform the magic immediately, *you might die.* You hurriedly push your chair away from her table and leave the building.

Rushing down the street, you feel your throat constrict. Could it be a killing fear, or is it an illness coming on that is destined to claim your life? Arousing the fury of the psychic has become yet another in a long series of disasters. Yes, a curse makes perfect sense. A cloud of doom now hangs over your head. Nothing you do seems to go right and the future seems utterly hopeless.

So you've been hexed. Or have you? Think about the motivations of the people involved. Perhaps the psychic was a phony who was just out to get your money. Perhaps your lover truly found a person who was a better fit. Maybe your job, which threw you into conflict with coworkers, wasn't really the best environment for you. Each circumstance on its own can make sense, but when put together, these events might convince you that a negative supernatural force is at work. Why did all those bad things happen at once? Is it something you're bringing upon yourself? Is it just happenstance? Or could there truly be a hex upon you? This book seeks to investigate the answer to the question, "Have you been hexed?" If the answer is yes, with the help of this book you will have a clear course to follow to remove the hex from yourself forever. If the answer is no, you'll be able to understand why bad things are happening, and learn how to work on reversing the trend.

Grab ahold of your emotions, it's going to be a bumpy ride.

Take a moment to acknowledge your feelings before you dive into this book. Hexes evoke a multitude of powerful emotions, all of which affect how you absorb information while reading and can also influence how a hex runs its course. It is natural to feel fearful, angry, incredulous, skeptical, betrayed, depressed, hopeless, or detached and apathetic if you are wondering if you've been hexed. In this book, I will address those feelings and the impulses that may arise from them, such as the desire to get back at the person who may have hexed you. If it turns out that the hex is self-imposed, or simply a run of bad luck and coincidences, your emotions will also come into play when reversing the trend in your life.

So prepare to be empowered repeatedly throughout this book, and to become well-armed for any situation. If you are hexed, you will be able to confirm your feelings, break the curse forever, and deal with your enemies accordingly. If you are not hexed, you will be able to understand why you wondered if you were hexed, why your life isn't going the way you want, and how to take immediate action to change things for the better. By the end of this book, you'll be well-equipped not only to deflect and deactivate any real or imagined hexes that should come your way, but also to prevent negative magic from affecting you and those you love. Draw on a source of inner strength and read on.

ONE

✕•◦◉◦•✕

So you think you've been hexed ...

So you think you've been hexed. Perhaps somebody has come straight out and told you that he or she has placed a curse on you. It could be an angry customer, an ex-lover, or a newly created enemy. Or, perhaps you've noticed an unusual string of misfortunes, such as a series of failed relationships, an inability to earn or save money, or a mysterious illness. Perhaps an enigmatic stranger has suddenly destroyed your marriage, luring your beloved away with what you can only assume to be black magic. Chances are that you feel violated, hopeless, helpless, angry, and afraid.

I have known many of those sorts of situations. The vast majority of them have been clients of mine, who had already seen me for fortune-telling services for help discovering their futures, confirming past mistakes, and empowering them to deal with present challenges. Many had come to me with specific concerns about hexes. And sometimes, even my own friends and family have come to me with the fear that a terrible curse had fallen upon them.

What is magic?

So what is this mysterious and sometimes spooky thing called magic? Magic, sometimes spelled "magick" to distinguish it from stage illusions, can be many things. Magic can be a prayer said while kneading bread. It can be found in a friendship bracelet, a curse muttered under the breath, a song, a dance, or a long and complicated ritual. The one thing that characterizes magic is that its purpose is to produce a result desired by the practitioner. With such a broad definition, magic is something done by people every day. Indeed, it is impossible to live life without magic. This book will explore magic throughout history and across cultures, especially as it relates to malicious magic like hexes.

What is a hex?

A hex is any form of magic used with intent to cause harm, either spiritual, emotional, mental, or physical. Since a hex is defined by its desired outcome, the methodology for casting such curses and the manner in which they are implemented can vary widely. Common ways of casting hexes can include words spoken aloud, the harming of animals or insects, the use of dolls or other images, elaborate rituals, or simple glares and gestures. Hexes can be placed on people, animals, objects, places, and even events. Hexes can affect one person, a relationship, or even an entire family line. Some hexes affect a person instantaneously and disappear as quickly as they take effect. Other curses run their course over a month, years, or even generations.

Perhaps the most common and therefore most troublesome kind of hex is one that a person places on himself or herself unwittingly. A self-imposed curse can be very destructive and challenging to remove. Luckily, any type of hex can be removed. Better still, any kind of hex can be prevented, and this book will explain how to avoid being hexed, and how to cure a curse should one arise.

How black magic works

In this time of high emotion, it important to educate yourself about the reality of black magic and how it works. Knowledge of a hex's basic mechanisms will help you to avoid wasting time or energy when dismantling them. Being informed can also help you to identify opportunistic thieves who may try to take advantage of you during this vulnerable time. Let's start with the history of malicious magical practices, and advance through current magical philosophy so you can understand the big picture.

History

Long before war declarations were penned, hexes were scratched on stone or lead. The modern definition of magic, attributed to Aleister Crowley, is "the science and art of causing change to occur in conformity with the will." I think it's pretty safe to say that before the first human being ever hit or kicked another person, he or she was wishing the enemy ill.

In ancient Egypt, Greece, and Rome, curses were in their heyday. Written curses as well as bound or pierced figures were common magical techniques. The Romani people needed no such props to tell a cursed story, and Arabs needed only a malevolent stare to employ the "evil eye" on an enemy. Across cultures and regions, many different techniques have been used throughout history, however, all subscribe to specific laws of magic, which were detailed by Isaac Bonewits in 1971.

LAWS OF MAGIC

Some laws of magic are more relevant to detecting, preventing, and breaking curses than others. The Law of Knowledge and the Law of Names explain that, for the person who hexes you, knowing your personal details, including strengths and weaknesses as well as all names by which you are known, increases his or her degree of control. If a person knows nothing about you, this can seriously limit their ability to hex.

The Laws of Synchronicity and of Association dictate that patterns are often required in magic, and can aid hex detection if you notice a pattern of negativity in your life directly synchronized to specific times or events, or associated with people or objects. For example, if you notice that the effects of your suspected hex get worse whenever a specific enemy is around, during every waning moon, or every time you hear a frog's croak, these patterns may be consistent with evidence of a real hex. If you can detect no such patterns, their lack indicates that your bad luck may not be due to a hex after all.

The Law of Similarity and Law of Contagion are behind the similarity of props used in black magic as well as many other forms of magic. If you find objects that are similar to you or your predicament—for example, a maimed doll that looks like you, a defaced photograph of yourself, or a drawing of an injury or mishap that has befallen you—these may have been used in a hex. The Law of Contagion means that things that have been connected to you emotionally or physically may be used in magic as well, such as hairs from a hat or hairbrush, a precious stuffed animal or ring, or a favorite article of clothing.

The Laws of Positive and Negative Attraction can draw your attention to what is happening in the life of the person you believe hexed you. If he or she is experiencing oddly similar misfortunes to you, such as a car wreck happening in the same week as yours, this can be due to magical repercussions. Conversely, if you find that you are losing money at the same time your enemy wins the lottery, or if all love prospects leave your life at the same time your enemy takes on dozens of lovers, this could be consistent with evidence of spell effects.

Modern cultures that curse

Just because the laws of magic work across cultures doesn't mean that hexes are prevalent in all cultures. Hexes are historically common. One hears of cursed objects, family curses, and black magic worked as a result of love triangles. But this doesn't mean that they are widespread in your own suburban neighborhood today.

It is important to know that in some regions and cultures, curses are not viewed as distasteful and silly. In some communities, black magic is as natural and expected when a loved one has been wronged as a phone call to the police, if not more so. Instead of picturing a mysterious, evil, cold-hearted spell-caster, consider that some humble individual who feels threatened or hurt by you may be the culprit, especially if you have been outside your country or culture recently.

For example, Thai, Hmong, Satanist, Hoodoo, and Vodou community members may feel they have little recourse besides spiritual protection from a real or imagined danger from an outsider. However, in a nation with a Christian or secular majority, you're unlikely to come across someone who practices hexing as a way of life. They are unlikely to be sitting on the bleachers of the opposing sports team or plotting against your political candidate. Hexes can indeed be real, but it is the goal of this book to point out just how rare—and manageable—they are.

TWO

—⟨⦁⊙⦁⟩—

HOW TO DETERMINE
IF YOU HAVE BEEN HEXED

Understanding hex detection

As you read in the introduction, the process of confirming a hex is not exact. A good analogy is the diagnosis of a mental illness. First, it is important to rule out other problems, like physical illness, that can aggravate or cause similar symptoms. Then a careful examination of the constellation of symptoms along with a few common screening questions can narrow down the likely diagnosis. It is possible to be wrong, and it is possible for the diagnosis to change over time. Likewise, if you discover a hex, it could be that your lack of experience has led you to an erroneous conclusion, or that the hex will eventually wear off on its own. Regardless of the answers you find, try not to panic. Even the worst hex can be removed, and this book will carefully instruct you on various methods that even the inexperienced can use.

How to confirm whether you have really been hexed

Say you've logically considered the evidence and determined that many signs indicating a hex are present, and very few or no pieces of evidence that reassure you that you haven't been hexed. Now you can move onward from the strictly logical approach and tap into your psychic intuitive understanding of what is happening to you.

Divination or psychic reading is one way to accurately determine the presence or absence of a hex. A psychic reading is the practice of using an understanding drawn from perception other than the five natural senses in order to determine answers about the past, present, or future. Divination is a type of psychic reading involving the use of divinatory tools such as tarot cards or a pendulum in order to receive a visual of your answer.

A potential problem with using psychic reading to determine whether a hex has been placed on yourself is that you are using the same brain to perform the psychic reading that thought there might be a hex in the first place. This bias can make you perceive signs or symptoms that aren't really there and ignore signs to the contrary. Psychic reading is also a skill that can take time and practice to perfect, so you can easily get a false positive simply out of a lack of experience or skill. For that reason, I will first give you tips for using another person as a psychic to check for the presence of a hex and give you a second opinion, and then go into a few divination options that you can perform on yourself that are the least likely to produce erroneous results.

Safely using a psychic reader

If you already know somebody with intuitive tendencies, your first reaction may be to go to them to see if they know what is going on. If your psychic friend or family member already knows you suspect a hex, be aware that the same bias might subconsciously affect them as well. It is easier for your loved one to get worked up about the same fear and confirm something that you already think is true than to dispel fears head on and try to convince you of the opposite. If possible, seek an unbiased third-party psychic, someone who doesn't know about your troubles and woes, like a friend of a friend or a professional.

If hiring a professional psychic, do your best to find one locally in your town, one you can meet in person. As with any other professional, you should be able to ask for references. Don't worry about insulting a psychic in making a friendly request for professional references; a reputable psychic should be proud and happy to provide you with evidence that he or she has helped other satisfied customers.

Before going to your appointment, ask the professional psychic if he or she has ever discovered a hex on a client in the past. If so, ask what he or she offers to do when that happens. It is okay for a psychic to want payment for the reading regardless of whether you have a curse or not, because their time is valuable even if your reading tells you that you're just fine and dandy. If a psychic already has a lineup of hex-breaking products to sell you, or if he or she will not answer your question or tries to scare you over the phone into coming in immediately, hang up and go to another psychic instead.

For example, as a professional psychic, I will perform readings for those who believe that they may have been hexed, and I do require compensation for my time and efforts even if it turns out that there was no hex at all, which occurs in the vast majority of cases. However, I gladly tell my clients before their readings that if I do discover a curse, I will offer to remove it or give instructions for self-removal at no extra charge. Don't expect anyone to do a preemptive hex removal before doing a reading to verify that a curse is even present. It would be a waste of everyone's time to offer hex removal to everyone who thought they might be cursed. To do so would certainly leave a professional no other time or energy with which to earn a living.

Using divination yourself to confirm or deny the presence of a hex

There are several signs that you can look for using divination systems searching for evidence consistent with the presence of a curse, or evidence that confirms that no curse is present at all. The best time to use divination is during a full moon, which maximizes natural psychic ability. I suggest you use more than one method to check for a curse since, as explained earlier, your own fears or personal bias may make it easy for you to jump to a conclusion or a false positive. If you see one or more reassuring signs, it is safe to say that the curse is either entirely imagined, self-imposed, or simply a run of bad luck. These kinds of trends can be managed, and a later chapter in this book will offer methods to deal with them.

Using palmistry to check for a curse

In the past, before palmistry books were available to the public, scamming psychics would gasp in horror if they spied a star in the palm of the hand. These are shapes made up of tiny lines anywhere in the palm that look like an asterisk, pentagram, or Star of David. The ruse of the star in the palm was effective because actually, it was based in truth. A star can represent focused energy and conflict—up to and including a hex. However, a star in the palm is not always a hex or even bad news. In fact, a star under the ring finger can mean fame and fortune, along with the metaphorical "curse" that comes along with those blessings. Moreover, most people don't go an entire lifetime without having a star appear in their palm at some point, possibly fading over time when the powerful life event subsides. Nonetheless, a star in the palm is an important piece of evidence to seek when investigating a potential curse. The presence of a star in the palm does not *absolutely* confirm a hex, but the absence of a star in the palm *can* confirm that you are not hexed at all.

Look for an asterisk, Star of David, or pentagram made up of small lines, especially on your life line, the large, major line that wraps in a graceful curve around your thumb. Another especially likely place to see a star that represents a curse is on or near your lunar mount, the fleshy part on the lower half of the percussive edge of your palm, the side of your hand that you would use to perform a karate chop. Both of those areas have to do with the spirit realm, magic, and your life energy. Stars present elsewhere are more likely to be naturally occurring conflict in your life.

Using a pendulum to check for a curse

A pendulum is a plumb bob, an object allowed to swing freely on a string or a chain. When used for divination purposes, it can be an obvious extension of your internal psychic knowledge, made external so that you can clearly see yes or no answers. You can buy a pendulum or make one by hanging a ring on a string.

To use your pendulum, go to a private space and relax to focus your attention. Since a nervous or overwhelmed mind can make your hands shake and your results inconclusive, now is a good time to practice grounding. Grounding is a practice by which excess or stuck energy—the life force that flows through you and is responsible for magic as well as your emotional and spiritual state of being—is allowed to flow harmlessly into the earth. Healthy energy is then drawn back into your body, giving you a calm but alert state of mind.

Begin by closing your eyes and visualizing your energy, which you may experience as a feeling of exhaustion or jittery anxiety at times when grounding is most needed. You can visualize energy in your mind's eye as water, light, smoke, tree roots, shiny beads, or anything else you can imagine in movement. Notice whether the energy gathers in any particular place in your body, if it seems to be moving quickly or slowly, or if the energy is dark or faded. Let the energy flow out through the soles of your feet into the earth, and allow fresh energy to flow upward back into your body at the same time, flushing away any sense of tiredness or edginess until it is in gentle motion throughout your body in your mind's eye. More about grounding will come later, since a lack of proper grounding can play a big role in creating symptoms that can mimic the presence of a hex.

When you feel ready, hold your pendulum in your dominant hand between your thumb and forefinger, and drape it over the back of your fingers, lifting your pinkie finger slightly so that the end can swing freely from that finger. If possible, wait until you can hold still enough for the pendulum to be stationary, although if your hands are naturally shaky, this is not necessary. Ask your pendulum, "Show me what 'yes' looks like," and then wait until a clear pattern of motion is established. This may be a swinging back and forth, a clockwise circle, or a counterclockwise circle. Thank the pendulum and attempt to return back to the baseline, as stationary as possible. Ask the pendulum, "Show me what 'no' looks like." Wait until a clearly different pattern of movement is shown. Each pendulum can be unique in how answers are displayed, so it is a good habit to perform this calibration before any pendulum reading.

Now is the moment of truth. Ask your pendulum if you are currently under the influence of malicious magic such as a curse or a hex, and wait for the answer. Note the first pattern of movement you see, as that is your answer—even if the movement changes after a bit of time passes. Keep in mind that the pendulum is not moving on its own; it is simply magnifying your own expression of inner knowledge. As a result, a false positive is a possibility.

USING TAROT CARDS TO CHECK FOR A CURSE

If you are already familiar with the decks of seventy-eight cards used to tell fortunes, you may be more comfortable using them for divination than other tools. However, obviously tarot cards are limited since there is no single card with a picture of your enemy on it and a confirmation of a curse or hex. In fact, if there was a one in seventy-eight chance of getting a curse card pulled in a reading, everyone would tend to avoid using tarot cards due to their inaccuracy and tendency to frighten the reader. Certainly some tarot cards are challenging, and some have little positive to say. But when somebody's reading consists entirely of the more negative cards, it's easy to conclude that everything is not going all that well in that person's life. A completely negative reading, although rare, would be consistent with someone who is suffering the effects of a hex.

In particular, when cards of the suit of swords, which indicate conflict, are drawn almost to the exclusion of any other suit, this can point to an individual who is cursed. For example, the Nine of Swords can be consistent with somebody who is losing sleep due to an enemy attempting to hex or appear in his or her dreams. The Ten of Swords can also indicate the feeling of being overwhelmed and helpless, which often accompanies a hex. The Three of Swords would likely be present in the case of one whose love life is the target of a curse. The Seven of Swords can be a card indicative of malicious magic when associated with other signs.

If most or all of the fives show up in a tarot reading, that is a sign of the instability and loss that can be the goal of most hexes. Pay attention to the major arcana, the twenty-two most powerful cards in the deck. These are the cards you would not find in a regular playing-card deck. Their presence would be warranted in a curse reading since they represent powerful energies, especially when one is at a crossroads in life. No single card can represent a curse with clarity, but some major arcana cards, especially when reversed, can be more telling than others. In particular, pay attention if any of the following cards show up: the Moon, associated with cycles, deception, and fear; the High Priestess, associated with magic; the Death card, associated with endings and loss (but *not* actual death!); the Devil for self-imposed curses and obsession; and the Lovers, which can mean one's own passions getting the better of them. All these cards are worthy of attention.

In summary, there is no single tarot card that tells you you're cursed. But if you were to get all of the fives in the deck, most of the suit of swords, and a few revealing major arcana cards, the reading would suggest a major negative life change that might be associated with a curse. Tarot cards aren't the best tool for determining the presence or absence of a curse, and they're certainly not a required tool. I include the use of tarot cards here simply due to their popularity; if a reader is already a skilled tarot practitioner and feels comfortable using them for the purpose of hex detection, they can make a useful addition.

The limitations of the tarot cards aren't always a problem, however. I remember one case in which a client came to me believing a family curse had carried forward from a past life. He didn't tell me before the reading, but he had done extensive meditation sessions in order to do past-life regressions. In dreams and in a trance state, he had already traveled back in time to the point in history at which he believed his family had acquired the curse, and simply wanted to come to me for confirmation with tarot cards. When I drew ten cards for him, I managed to draw all four kings from the seventy-eight-card deck. I began to interpret the kings for him, and his eyes were wide with shock. It turned out that he had experienced a past life with the warring of four rival small kingdoms that had ended in a family curse. The four kings staring at him from the table were clear confirmation to him that his past life and family line issues needed to be resolved.

Checking your aura for a curse

An aura is a halo of spiritual energy that surrounds you. It can be very useful to be able to perceive your own aura in order to notice changes that may be positive or negative, especially if the effects of a suspected curse are affecting a part of your body physically. Some people are able to observe an aura with their eyes or in the mind's eye as a colored light or cloud. Others perceive auras by sensing with their hands a soft resistance, or they may feel a fuzzy or tingling sensation. Still others don't detect a perception with their senses, but instead feel like they just *know* for certain where the boundaries are between the aura and the rest of the world. One can also use a pendulum to detect the boundary between one's aura and the rest of the world.

To attempt to perceive your aura, you'll need a mirror, a pendulum, and a quiet room in which you are alone. Make sure it has good lighting. You may wish to bring a journal to note your observations or a sheet of paper and some art supplies to draw your aura in color. It is best to try to see your first aura when you are alone, because sometimes proximity to other people can cause you to naturally withdraw your aura so that it is closer to your body and thus smaller and harder to see. In fact, you can try to blow it up bigger with a little visualization. Close your eyes and imagine you want to gain attention. You might imagine yourself as a movie star, as an actor on a stage, or as an attractive person trying to catch the eye of your crush from across the room at a party. Try to inflate your confidence and presence so you become a beacon of dynamic energy. Then, open your eyes and look at yourself in the mirror.

Relax your gaze so that your eyes are softly focused, as if you were looking past your image to somewhere behind your reflection in the mirror. Sit quietly for a few minutes and continue to gaze at the mirror without moving your eyes around too much. Your aura may slowly become perceptible as a lightness, a cloud, or a halo around your body. Note its thickness, any movement, colors (which may or may not appear), and whether there are any dark spots or places where your aura seems to be missing.

If you can't "see" your aura, try something else. With your hands, try to feel the area surrounding your body. See if you can feel a thickness in the air close to the body and try to determine its boundary. If you have no luck with this method, try using a pendulum. Dangle the pendulum just above one arm, holding it with the other hand. Start very close to the skin. Watch the pendulum's movement as you slowly draw it up, farther away from your arm. Usually there will be an obvious motion when you hold the pendulum within your aura's field, and then a cessation of motion or a drastic change in the nature of the motion when you cross the border of your aura. In this way, you can test the thickness of your aura over different parts of your body. The speed and amplitude of the pendulum's motion can indicate the intensity of color that some people can perceive visually. A healthy aura can change drastically in color and size throughout an ordinary day. In times of anxiety or exhaustion, your aura can be very thin and pale. When you are excited, energetic, and confident, your aura may be very thick and vibrant. The color may change due to your goals or your wellness throughout the day. This variability can make it hard for another person to tell from your aura whether you are cursed unless he or she is already familiar with how your aura usually looks and how it varies.

That being said, healthy auras have a few things in common. The thickness is relatively uniform throughout, although it is okay if it is thicker around the head or midsection. An especially thin spot is a warning flag, particularly if it is around the head or around a part of the body you suspect is affected by a curse.

Dark spots are also a red flag in auras, as they can represent stuck or blocked energy. Often a dark spot will appear during times of illness or injury around the affected body part, but dark spots can also be associated with a hex. Again, remember that things can change throughout the day; if you see a thin spot or dark spot, don't panic. They can be a part of the natural healing process from any illness or injury, or they might be transient because of a rough morning or a headache. Wait a few hours, eat a healthy meal, rest, and then try again. If you see the same phenomenon, you may wish to start some of the psychic protection methods described later in this book.

Clearly there are many tools that can help you, but remember that it's best to use more than one divination method when searching for affirmation of a hex.

Evidence that you are not hexed at all

Logically, it isn't enough to simply check off a few pieces of evidence that indicate you may have been hexed. You should also carefully and critically consider any evidence to the contrary. Perhaps a few odd things have happened to you lately that line up with the potential of a hex, but there are also glaringly obvious signs that you couldn't possibly be hexed. These signs should not be ignored. It can be hard to notice comforting evidence when you are feeling jumpy and fearful, but following is a list of some signs that, if true for you, should offer you reassurance that you are unlikely to have been hexed at all.

- *You exist in a community*
  where black magic is not commonplace
  Again, no matter how many television shows one watches about magic, witchcraft, or Satanism, somebody who is not deeply studied in the art, culture, and science of hexing is unlikely to be able to pull it off successfully.

- *Your enemy's life situation is generally*
  in disrepair and beyond his or her control
  So you think a powerful witch has cursed you, but you notice that he or she is sort of a loser without a job and his or her love life is devoid of joy. Surely

a great magician would be able to wield his or her magic to solve some of those life problems! Be very dubious about the hexing magical skills of someone who can't even seem to manage their own life problems.

- *There are no patterns surrounding the negativity in your life*
The Laws of Synchronicity and Association can give major clues as to a specific hexed object or place, along with the timing of how the person may have cursed you. A lack of patterns indicates that neither of those laws' effects are in action. So if you notice bad things happening at random, no matter what time of month it may be, what jewelry you might be wearing, or which people may be around, that negativity could be pure happenstance.

- *You can point to exceptions to the rule of your bad luck or misfortunes*
A truly effective curse can create misery that seems to be without escape; it never allows the target of its effects a moment's rest. Everyone has bad days, bad months, even bad years. Everyone's love life can have dry spells. If you can admit to yourself that you've had happy moments, joys, near successes, and small wins, it could be that you're just feeling down in the dumps instead of having an actual curse applied to your life.

- *You don't know when the perceived hex effects began*
  A hex always has a clear beginning. After all, if you
  have been cursed, prior to the curse you were not
  under the effects of negative magic at all. After a
  magically capable enemy takes a specific action that
  usually happens over the course of mere minutes
  or hours, the hex takes effect immediately. Even if
  a rare curse takes several days to perform, or is set
  for a specific timed release date in the future, there
  is a clear period before the effects begin and after.
  Curses don't slowly ramp up and gradually back off
  or increase effects as time marches on. If you don't
  notice a time before the curse happened to you or
  to your family, it may mean that you have always
  suffered from a natural depressed temperament that
  causes you to notice negative things.

- *You have been told that you've been hexed by a psychic who
  then offered to cure your condition for a large sum of money*
  Not all or even most professional psychics are crooks,
  but the natural fear of curses produces a scam that
  occurs often enough to warrant a warning. The most
  common scenario for this scam is a client visiting
  a psychic, perhaps after having a break-up with
  an ex or suffering a natural dry spell in romantic
  matters. The psychic gasps at some terrifying sign
  of a curse and offers a complicated set of rituals or
  cleansings to be performed that require an offering

of a large amount of money in order to work at all. Just as you might get a second opinion if a doctor or veterinarian told you that the only option was a costly and drastic treatment, it is important to be a cautious consumer and critical thinker when using a professional psychic, especially if you go looking for one to discuss a potential hex. Be extremely suspicious if you weren't the first to bring up the subject of a hex, or if the psychic offers you no other recourse to break the spell except by financial means, or threatens dire consequences if you want to walk out the door to think about it for a day. Never "loan" anyone money that you think will be given back after it is placed on an altar to a deity or used in a spell—you will never see that money again.

Evidence that a curse may have been placed on you

Before you run out to try to remove a hex, it is important to look for evidence that a real hex has been placed. This is because you can actually create negative effects upon yourself by continuously thinking that a hex is there when it does not exist, even as you're taking action to get rid of it. In effect, you could be hexing yourself. Therefore, be skeptical and cautious when considering the possibility of being hexed. A good place to start understanding hexes is with logic, since curses are quite rare. Here you'll see a few pieces of evidence that may indicate the presence of a real hex. If you have just one, it might be a coincidence or a mistake, but many factors piling up can add credence to your suspicions.

- *You have been told that you*
  have been cursed by a plausible enemy
  Your own mind is at work just as effectively as magic if you are convinced that something bad is going to happen to you. This "placebo effect bias" means that your enemy has nothing to lose and everything to gain by telling you that a hex has been placed upon you. Even if he or she is a terrible magician, at the very least he or she might make you worry and potentially affect yourself negatively. Note that just because somebody says they've cursed you doesn't mean it actually happened. Somebody who knows you have a fear of the occult or who has learned you are interested in dark subjects may try to capitalize on your anxieties with a lie.

- *You have recently been out of the country and*
  immersed in a culture where curses are commonplace
  As mentioned earlier, curses are relatively uncommon and unlikely in modern Western society. However, if you have recently traveled to a country where magic tends to replace or supplement religion and medicine, you are more likely to have been exposed to a person with the means to hex.

- *You've found defaced photos, bound or
  mutilated dolls, or dead animals or insects*
  The magical Law of Similarity is used in hexes that
  involve defaced photographs, bound or mutilated dolls,
  or creatures that are harmed in the hopes that similar
  effects will befall you. Of course, any angry ex is more
  likely than not to tear up an old photo, and animals
  die of natural causes all the time.

- *Low-value items close to you have been stolen from you*
  The magical Law of Contagion is used in curses that
  involve items that are emotionally or physically close
  to you. So if somebody were to break into your house,
  ransack the place, and bypass your electronics and
  jewelry in favor of stealing your comb, nail clippers,
  pillowcase, or a hat you wear every day, that would be
  suspicious.

- *An enemy is suffering similar misfortunes or
  suddenly making gains in life while you suffer losses*
  There are some systems of magical belief that
  propose that every action one takes in life, whether
  magical or otherwise, has a similar reaction upon
  the magical practitioner. This is called karma. So, if
  you get a mysterious and rare illness and your enemy
  or his or her child gets the same malady, you may
  be observing what could be karmic repercussions.
  Other systems of magic draw power or energy from
  other people, in what is sometimes called psychic

vampirism. When I use the term "energy" here, I do not mean energy in the scientific context, but in a spiritual one. Spiritual energy, sometimes called *chi,* is the life force that flows through the universe and all living things. It is the wellspring of magic. If you start losing all sources of income in your life while your enemy keeps having windfall after windfall, this would be consistent with an energy-draining psychic or magical link. Since these paired events can happen naturally in the universe, evidence of this nature is not as strong as the previous examples, but should be considered corroborative and added to other evidence.

THREE

×◄•◉•►×

WHAT IF I JUST HAVE BAD LUCK?

So what do you do if, after performing divination, you discover that you don't have a hex placed on you at all? The fact that a hex isn't affecting you does not invalidate any misery or undue misfortune that you may be experiencing in your life. When I perform a divination that reveals no hex is present, the client usually experiences a mixture of emotions—a wave of relief followed by a sense of denial, and awareness that something is *definitely* amiss. Even if convinced, the client may then feel embarrassed or ashamed for mistakenly believing a hex was responsible for his or her woes.

Firstly, don't feel bad about thinking there might have been a hex. As you can see from the chapter on confirming the presence of a hex, curses can actually be quite subtle and mysterious, so unless you were already an expert on malicious magic, it would be completely unlikely that you would be able to instantly recognize a curse or something like it. Secondly, there is no correlation between lack of intelligence and belief in an erroneous curse. I have seen brilliant professionals in many fields assume a hex when an obvious run of bad luck enters their lives. Just yesterday, a successful employee at a major software corporation approached me, begging to be a case study for this book due to a series of oddly terrible events that happened in his life.

Why might people assume hexes are to blame? And what can happen to people when they erroneously believe a hex has been placed? I'll answer these questions, and also help you understand what may actually be behind the real negative effects that you are seeing, and how to turn that bad luck around. I hope to validate the serious issue of bad luck and acknowledge that ignoring it may not necessarily see it go away on its own.

Why real and effective hexes are so rare, but perceived curses are so common

As discussed earlier, genuine and effective hexes are extremely rare in modern Western culture. Not only is it unlikely that your enemy would turn to black magic, but there is an extremely low probability that such a random enemy would also happen to have obtained the skill and years of discipline necessary to successfully hex you. Your average sullen teen-aged neighbor, angry that you caught him in an act of vandalism, or the angry ex-wife of a lover is more likely to resort to lies and emotional abuse than to a hidden reserve of real and dangerous magical power.

Even so, many people are under the misperception that they have been hexed. The issue may not be obvious to most, since many people keep their fear of a hex secret from friends and family. I'm aware because it is one of the top questions I'm asked as a fortune-teller, right after questions on other everyday life problems like relationship strife and career advancement. Regardless of their rarity, hexes are on the forefront of peoples' minds because we tend to be collectors and categorizers of all kinds of information, especially as it pertains to positive and negative events in our lives.

What mental habits, evolutionarily based or learned, lead people to such beliefs?

It is natural to draw connections between events, whether they seem related or not. In fact, if your brain didn't strive to make connections where none were present, there would be something wrong with you. The natural trait of making associations is a survival instinct found in many species, but especially in such intelligent animals as humans. If you were to eat a melon left out of the refrigerator and then suffer violent illness the next day, you would naturally assume that you have food poisoning. Even dogs and rats will make the same associations between foods and illness in order to survive potentially dangerous food sources. As a perceptive and survival-motivated person, when a terrible event happens in your life such as a car accident or a divorce, your brain will naturally start searching for causes in order to prevent further injury. The more varied and numerous negative events become, the more impossible it may be to correlate the true source of the problem, as it may actually be a combination of many factors.

The natural, evolutionary trait of making connections often leads to erroneous conclusions, spawning an entire field of psychology surrounding cognitive bias. Cognitive bias is an erroneous interpretation drawn from a pattern of abnormal judgment. The adaptive trait of making quick decisions becomes a liability when it comes to making the wrong choices about hexes. Nobody is free from cognitive bias, no matter their level of education, but it may help to know that some common cognitive biases affect us all, so don't beat yourself up about them when they occur.

Anchoring: Sometimes people get fixated on one negative event, which causes them to ignore all the following positive events that prove they are not hexed. For example, if you just suffered a break-up, you're probably feeling pretty gloomy and unlovable, causing you to ignore that attractive person who is trying to flirt with you from across the room. It may be easier to think that your love life is cursed than to notice the ray of sunshine on a cloudy day.

Attentional bias: If a hex is more emotionally arresting than other potential sources of the problem, you can easily be drawn to think that is the only potential solution. For example, if you were suffering a long-term illness and worried about having been hexed, you might keep thinking about that instead of the more boring (but likely) scenarios of a virus, allergy, or the environmental factors and lifestyle choices that were making you unhealthy.

Availability heuristic: This bias appeals to the most emotionally charged or recent memory as the most likely explanation. If your ex-girlfriend screams at you that she has cast an evil spell on you as she storms out the door, when you stub your toe later you might blame the curse, even if you frequently stub your toe on the same table and know that your ex-girlfriend can't even follow the microwave instructions on a bag of vegetables, much less cast an effective hex.

Clustering illusion: People tend to think that coincidences are rare, but in random sets of data there are often surprising runs and clusters of information. So if you got in a traffic jam twice in the same day and you think surely it must be a curse, you might be underestimating the normal frequency of that event.

Confirmation bias: The fact that you are reading this book might be evidence of your own confirmation bias, which is the tendency people have to seek out information that confirms rather than disproves their beliefs.

Conservatism: Even though you just disproved a hex, do you find yourself still believing in it against all your better judgment? That's because it is natural for our brains to be slow to take on a new belief even in the face of overwhelming evidence.

Contrast effect: Imagine you've had a pretty good day when traffic was light on the way to work, you were complimented on your appearance by an attractive person, and you find yourself being particularly productive. Suddenly, you spill coffee all over your white shirt and declare that you are having a bad day. When a contrasting incident wipes out your ability to logically recall previous evidence, you are experiencing the contrast effect.

Empathy gap: People tend to underestimate the role feelings play in decision making, and being the likely victim of a hex would naturally be an emotionally charged situation. Even if you think you have a cool head when evaluating information, your emotions may get the best of you.

Focusing effect: Bad luck and bad days tend to seem worse because of the focusing effect. If you've had a streak of negative events, you're more likely to predict that only more bad stuff is going to happen in the future. Unfortunately, the result is that either more bad stuff happens or you are more likely to notice it.

Framing effect: The framing effect is at work if a crooked person selling supposed hex cures or an angry enemy claims that you are hexed even when you are not. When your life is presented with a different frame, one in which you suppose a hex, all of the bad events that you normally correctly identify as normal may suddenly seem supernatural.

Frequency illusion: Imagine that a demanding customer at work named Susan yells at you that you are cursed. Suddenly, you start noticing the name Susan everywhere. It appears on a television game show, on the radio, and you meet two more Susans that very same day. Was Susan a powerful magician to make this happen? No, but frequency bias tends to make us notice something "everywhere" that we might have previously ignored.

Illusion of validity: If the evidence of a hex is consistent enough, you might believe it, even if that evidence is very weak. For example, a friend of mine thought he was hexed because his refrigerator died and his turtle tank setup wasn't working either. As the small negative events added up, he reached a conclusion even though, from the outside looking in, anyone else would think it was unlikely that somebody had gone through the trouble to work magical powers to affect his refrigerator motor and turtle tank.

Illusory correlation: Illusory correlation is at the heart of many curse suppositions. For example, if a person were to suffer storm damage to his house right after being dumped by his girlfriend, he might think those two events were somehow related, even though they clearly are not. From an illusory correlation, it is only one more jump to the conclusion that a hex has been placed.

Jealousy bias: The majority of cases of mistaken hexes I've seen are ones in which an ex's "other woman" or "other man" is blamed. Jealousy bias causes us to believe that the person who stole away our beloved is dangerous, personally attacking us, or more powerful than us.

Just world hypothesis: Sometimes well-meaning friends or relatives might suggest you are cursed. People tend to believe that the world is generally good, and that bad things don't happen to good people. So if you suffer an incredible loss, it may easily be assumed that some supernatural force, perhaps even a hex, caused you to be visited by such a tragedy.

Negativity bias: Crucial to assuming an erroneous hex, negativity bias causes you to ignore all the little good things that happen and to collect the data about bad events instead.

Pareidolia: Everyone can see shapes in the clouds in the sky even if they are just random formations of water vapor, but this natural ability can make the world seem more mystical than it actually is. When a hex is assumed, your mind sees or hears threatening messages in random sights and sounds.

Pessimism bias: Some people assume bad things will happen to them even if nothing truly bad has yet occurred. For such people, if a hex can possibly occur in the world, it will happen to them.

Restraint bias: We all assume that we have more willpower than we actually have. So if you find yourself overeating or cheating on a mate, it is easier to assume that somebody is controlling your behavior with a hex than to concede to your own weakness.

Selective perception: If you expect that a hex is going to cause you to have a bad day, then you may perceive that to be the case even when absolutely nothing bad happens that day.

Suggestibility: Unfortunately, all people have the potential to mistake what somebody has said as an actual experienced memory. When unscrupulous people suggest that a person may have been hexed, it is possible to acquire that truth as a false memory.

Curse scams and curse lies

As you learned above, anyone can become a "victim" of a curse scam through natural, human, cognitive biases like the framing effect and suggestibility. Well aware of the common phenomenon of mistaken hexes, some unscrupulous people even set up shop to take financial advantage of this. They advertise hex removal services for a large and ongoing cost. Some of the wilier ones even set up a trap, advertising the ability to reunite lovers or cure illnesses. Somehow they always find that a hex or unclean aura is the barrier.

As much as I don't want to have to write about the despicable practice of curse scams run by psychics, I have seen enough of their frightened clients to know that it happens more than it should. The fact that curse scams by psychics exist doesn't mean that all psychics are liars and scammers any more than the existence of lying lawyers or scamming mechanics means that you should avoid all people who fix cars or help with legal matters. However, please take care to read the section in this book on using psychic readers safely to be a careful consumer if you do choose to consult with a psychic.

Who misidentifies circumstances as a hex and why?

It may be tempting to think that only idiots can be fooled by curse scams or cook up an imaginary hex all on their own. However, it can happen to intelligent and successful people from all walks of life, across varied careers and age groups. I would even venture to say that most of the people who came to me mistakenly thinking they were hexed were more intelligent and capable than average.

The type of person who assumes a hex seems to have several positive traits that turn out to be his or her worst enemies. A resourceful person who excels in networking in business might be more likely to accidentally stumble across a professional who runs a curse scam. Quick-minded people who make creative connections and solve problems easily are more likely to jump to erroneous conclusions about hexes. Finally, almost everyone I have met who has assumed a hex is a deep thinker, someone who tends to ruminate about life issues and can sometimes overcomplicate problems as a result.

How a person can curse themselves

When I was a small child and would endlessly voice my worries and complaints about not being good enough at school or sports, my mother would point out that thoughts were things, and that if you think something is true long enough, you can make it so. At the time, I filed it away in my mind along with other myths, like if you cross your eyes long enough they'll stay that way. But it turns out that through cognitive biases and habits of mind, the similar warning that if you frown or pout too much your face will stay that way is more true than not.

Psychology and magic are inextricably intertwined. Many of the magic rituals already described in this book involve visualizing the flow of energy in the mind's eye in order to control the actual, external world. Energy clings to and follows your thoughts through your life, gathering more energy and more attention as it moves, as evidenced scientifically through cognitive biases like the focusing effect.

In particular, the magical Law of Attraction acts as an ancient and powerful spell that people practice unwittingly every day. The more that you think negative thoughts about your life and your future, or the more that you assume you have been hexed, the more these cognitive biases will make your thoughts into strongly held beliefs. Then the magical Law of Attraction will move energy to create those beliefs as truths in your real life. The degree of power your mind has over your life circumstances can be empowering if you make yourself aware of the process as it is happening. Conversely, you do have the power to unknowingly "curse" yourself with bad luck through habits of mind alone.

The sort of "curse" I'm talking about is when you unknowingly curse yourself with bad luck. It does not requires a complicated hex removal, although prayer never hurts. However, I liken it to a "curse" here metaphorically only to underscore the important point that the bad luck your mind can bring into your life is not just imaginary, but very tangible and distressing. Unfortunately, the common advice to just ignore it may not work to make it go away if you have strong habits of mind.

Through the power of the magical Law of Attraction, your mere thoughts have the power to make the difference between wealth and poverty when searching for a job, between a soul mate connection and eternal loneliness when seeking love, and even between life and death when fighting an illness or serious injury. Do not be afraid of your brain's power over your life, but don't take it lightly, either. A gloomy outlook on life isn't something normal that should be ignored if your mind is powerful enough to create bad luck. You must take action to empower yourself.

How to stop the habit of perpetuating bad luck or imagining curses

The good news is that just as there are a myriad of ways to begin the downward spiral into bad luck or imagined curses, there are many ways to bring yourself back out of your rut. I will explore several strategies to eliminate bad luck, from the practical and the physical, moving through the psychological and emotional, and finally making some spiritual suggestions. Feel free to try as many tactics as seem to work for you, since all of these can be healthy at any point in time.

Practical and physical solutions

Remember that there are serious medical problems that can mimic the effects of curses and possession. Beyond such simple cases of self-misdiagnosis, the body, mind, and spirit are so linked that physical problems can easily cause mental and spiritual issues. If you consistently experience bad luck that seems to be spiritual in nature, one of your first steps should be to visit a general physician for a check-up. In fact, though you can cherry-pick through most of the solutions in this chapter, I suggest that you don't make a physical medical check-in optional.

I don't intend to scare you unless it will mobilize you into action, but since I am one of those people who avoids going to the doctor, it is worth pointing out that chronic illnesses can turn serious and even deadly when they affect breathing. They can become acutely debilitating when you are driving or performing an activity during which you could fall and kill yourself. Seizure disorders can mimic "missing time" experiences as well as create hallucinations that could easily lead a person to believe that he or she was possessed, and if a seizure hit when the person was driving, it could be deadly to more than just him or her. Brain tumors and organ failures can cause similar effects and have the additional symptoms of lethargy and personality changes that can contribute to very real experiences of bad luck.

I must mention the potential presence of mental illness, which I place in this section because of the very real physiological component that a sufferer cannot simply wish away. People with emerging psychosis or who are developing a serious mental illness like schizophrenia are not the only ones who cultivate or imagine curse or possession-like symptoms. In fact, it is more commonly those with nonpsychotic struggles, like undiagnosed or poorly managed depression or anxiety, whom I have seen challenged with bad luck. Even if you are already in treatment for a mental disorder when you try to change your bad luck for the better, know that you will need to return to your therapist or medication prescriber immediately to work in concert with your physical and mental healing or maintenance. Your body, mind, and soul must all work harmoniously together in order to rid yourself of bad luck for good.

Although mental problems are very real, sometimes one can snap out of a funk or cycle of negativity simply by making proper nutrition, sleep, and exercise a priority in life. Natural chemical changes that occur when the body is well rested and healthy can boost a person's mood and have a direct effect on spiritual energy through the connection between the body and the mind. No amount of healthy lifestyle will eliminate a real problem with mental illness or a spiritual curse, but in the absence of such factors, a healthier way of life can precipitate a better outlook on life.

Psychological and emotional solutions

Even perfectly healthy people can have habits of mind that can foster bad luck life patterns. In fact, everyone has the potential to create bad luck through those natural cognitive biases mentioned earlier. Since cognitive biases are normal and impossible to eliminate entirely from life, I will only briefly draw your attention to negative habits of mind, but mainly focus on ways to prevent or mitigate them in a proactive manner.

CATCH YOURSELF THINKING
NEGATIVELY AND REWRITE THE SCRIPTS

We all talk to ourselves internally, and sometimes that monologue can get rather depressing if it picks up a negative pattern. Intelligent people especially tend to ruminate on mistakes they make, which keeps them up at night replaying negative scenarios in their heads. Negative self-talk that emerges from such mistakes can immediately bring about bad luck through the magical Law of Attraction as well as through cognitive biases. If low self-esteem and a sad or angry internal narrative sound like you, I have to praise you for the laudable quality of taking responsibility for the bad things that happen in your life instead of ignoring them or thinking they're somebody else's problem. You don't have to give up your sense of personal ownership of your problems, but you should be empowered to rewrite those scripts to get your life and your luck moving forward in a positive way, instead of spinning your wheels.

A client came to me with the insistence that he had been cursed to never find love. He had an impressive story of the many, many women who had scammed him for money and then left him. At the outset, the curse may have sounded genuine—he had quite a long line of failures in love. However, when I pressed him for details, I found out that the situation was not as it had seemed. The man was deaf, and he had gone through life assuming that he would never find love with a hearing woman. As a result, he had fallen prey to a succession of emails from Nigerian financial scammers who claimed to be beautiful deaf women. Instead of thinking that he could find love nearby with either hearing or deaf women, he had written himself a script that it would be difficult to find love. Unfortunately for him, he inadvertently made sure that the script came true. It turned out that he didn't have a true curse at all. He just needed to rewrite his internal scripts. Perhaps you have similar scripts that need rewriting.

For example, if you are working on a difficult assignment on the job or at school and telling yourself, "I suck at this," you are likely to make it true. Instead, catch yourself any time you think or say "I suck at this," and replace it with a more positive phrase such as "I am improving at this." Even if you don't feel that your improvement is true at the time, if you say it enough, you will improve. Some people aren't comfortable lying to themselves, and that's okay too. Try replacing the phrase with a positive but true statement like, "I am working hard at this" until you get more comfortable with rewriting your life's script.

Another good example is a repetitive negative thought about another person. If, every time you see a specific co-worker or client, you think "I hate him," then it will certainly be true, and you will only hate him more. Worse still, you'll find yourself attracting more hated and hateful people into your life. If you have a strong enough force of will to overcome your hate, try replacing that internal script with "I like him" whenever you catch yourself. If you can't bring yourself to go that far in the opposite direction, try to find one attribute that you do like about that person. "I like the way he always knocks before entering my office, and how he looks so relaxed when he sits in a chair," or even "I like his eye color and the tie he picked out today."

The worst terms in your mental lexicon are "always" and "never" when these extremes turn into negative self-talk. Catch yourself whenever you use extremes in an unhelpful way, such as "I will never find true love" or "I always mess up my relationship with my folks." Erase words like "always" and "never" from your negative vocabulary if you can, and replace the entire phrase that you keep repeating to yourself with something more hopeful and with room for exceptions from what you have experienced to be the rule, even if it is "I am lovable and I love my dog" or "I'm sure getting better at not picking fights with my folks than I was when I was a teenager!"

FOCUS ON EMPOWERING
SOLUTIONS INSTEAD OF BLAME

If things are going wrong in your life, you probably have the right to whine about it and nobody can blame you. The vast majority of clients who come to me with a case of bad luck are stuck in a cycle of circumstances and people around them making life unbearable. In such cases, self-blame is the last thing needed. However, taking a little ownership and responsibility where it is due can have the opposite of a depressive effect, allowing a person to see what can be changed amidst the huge mess of things that are beyond their control.

If you find yourself consistently blaming others, such as an ex, a family member, the economy, or a boss, stop yourself. Even if your blame is righteous, it does nothing to solve the problem or to empower you. Rewrite those negative scripts, as instructed above, and also work on finding the small things you can change in each situation that give you a sense of responsibility. The most resilient of people who have overcome difficult life challenges don't do so by asking "why me"— instead, they open themselves up to greater duties and opportunities for growth.

A client of mine believed that his life was cursed because he noticed many things acting up the same time. Several appliances in his house stopped working at once and his kitchen remodel job wasn't getting finished because he had lost his inspiration to continue working on it. Worst of all, he observed that he was overweight and didn't feel up to the sorts of physical activities and social situations that he would enjoy if he felt more confident in himself. From where he sat, it seemed like all of these bad things were happening to him, and his feelings of sadness and frustration were valid. However, from the outside looking in, you can see that all of his troubles were under his control. He could try diet and exercise to improve his weight, hire a contractor to finish the kitchen, and simply replace the broken appliances. He neglected to notice the good things in his life, like his high-income job and loving girlfriend, who was also a client of mine.

BEWARE THE COMPANY YOU KEEP

The attitudes of those around you can indirectly or directly influence your mood and luck. This category of solution borders on the spiritual due to a particular type of person called a "psychic vampire." In the same way that the vampires of myth feed on blood to survive, a person who is a psychic vampire learns to cope with a lack of spiritual energy by draining it from others, often without consent. In some cases, the influence of others is obvious, such as the case of an adult child staying at home for too long and leeching off his parents while enjoying a life of drugs and freedom from responsibility. In other cases of psychic vampirism, the effects can be more subtle, such as a friend whose visits always leave you feeling exhausted and blue. In between are those whose negative influences are entirely mental, like the husband who whines and complains all the time, or the gossiping aunt who leaves you feeling bad about yourself after you stoop to her level.

The naturally strong effects of relationships on your mind, body, and spirit are why so many of my clients experience hex-like effects surrounding a break-up. The negativity of a resentful partner can easily permeate more mundane parts of life, causing an undeniable slump of bad luck in both peoples' lives. After a break-up, depression or even an immediate relief from negative effects may cause a person to assume that an ex has been using black magic.

When a decision has been reached to break up, a new and separate identity for yourself should be affirmed or established and, if it is necessary to stay in contact at all, a new and more distant association with your ex should be clearly negotiated by setting firm limits and expressing closure. Some people find that the emotional hurt of drawing such a firm line can be too intense, so they choose to leave the door open for potential reconciliation. Unfortunately, for couples with binding energetic ties, or when one partner is a psychic vampire or a negative person in general, bad luck can follow for both people involved. Consider whether it is more kind to fully release your ex by choosing not to allow the possibility that you might get back together in the future. Even if a reunion would be technically possible, you can firmly decide to remove that scenario from your destiny and save both of you grief by telling your ex firmly and with a sense of finality to release you both forever.

Some of the tips and tricks on hex prevention you'll learn in chapter 6 may help you to mitigate the effects of a negative person if he or she can't be avoided or confronted directly, as in the case of a small child, a mother-in-law, or your boss's boss. However, the best solution is to limit the time and effort you devote to people who are not a positive influence in your life by setting appropriate boundaries and communicating your concerns directly. Even if the worst psychic vampire in your life is a beloved family member, setting aside time for yourself to recharge your personal batteries and laying down specific examples of how you would like to interact and communicate with him or her can give you some much needed breathing room to overcome your streak of bad luck.

GET A PHILOSOPHICAL PERSPECTIVE

It is easier said than done, but sometimes living more in the moment can help remove perceived barriers from your past and obstacles that loom in your future. Likewise, considering that the most challenging people in your life may be there for a purpose, as your greatest teachers, can make interactions with them seem less hopeless. Unfortunately, wishing that you could think with a philosophical perspective doesn't always make it true, unless you are a seriously convincing script re-writer. However, some of the more spiritual solutions below, such as meditation, can help you live in the moment as well as come to an enlightened perspective on why certain people and situations continue to repeat for you. In my belief system, our purpose here on earth is to learn, so even when things get incredibly difficult, I look forward to coming to the end of the lesson at some point and am hopeful that such tough instruction won't have to be repeated in my next life.

Spiritual solutions

So far, this book has focused on prayer as the spiritual solution to nearly every problem, and it works against bad luck as well. However, there are other spiritual practices that can enrich your life so as to leave no room for bad luck to take hold in the first place, or to crowd out the bad luck that has taken over your life like so many weeds in a garden. Just as your relationships with others border on the spiritual, many spiritual solutions border on the physical and mental realms.

THE LAW OF ATTRACTION

As was mentioned earlier, the magical Law of Attraction, or the principle that like energies attract like, can be used in the process of creating a hex. By the same logic, the Law of Attraction can create bad luck when bad luck becomes your life's focus. However, you can also wield this law as a tool to attract good luck, love, and abundance into your life. Like spiritual cleansing, this is deceptively simple, since it is essentially just the power of positive thinking. However, I have placed the Law of Attraction in the spiritual solutions section because I'd like you to step beyond simply rewriting your scripts to the best possible paraphrasing of your situation. I would like you to have the ability to create a positive scenario that does not yet exist.

Using daily affirmations as chants is one way to put the Law of Attraction into magical practice. The trick is to fully visualize and describe the outcome you desire as if it has already happened. It may feel disingenuous to lie to yourself about already having love, money, a job, or good luck. However, using the Law of Attraction is more than just faking it until you make it. In fact, you are using your own magical power to create the scenario you want as a reality on a spiritual level. In New Age terms, the astral plane is a sort of parallel spiritual dimension on which a potential future is built. Before a baby is born, for example, he or she exists on the astral plane. Likewise, when you visualize a doodle you are about to draw, or a conversation you are about to have, you begin to create its potential on the astral plane before it manifests here in reality.

To create an affirmation, move your concerns from the negative to the positive and into the present tense. For example, if you find yourself bemoaning that your job search is cursed, first rewrite that script from "I will never get a job" to "I want to get a job." From here, magical practitioners are tempted to use wording such as "a good job is coming my way!" Such positive and forward thinking is a step in the right direction, but to use the Law of Attraction and to manifest the job on the astral plane, try using an authoritative present tense such as "I have the perfect job." Visualize yourself firmly in your mind as content, wealthy, and enjoying your desired line of work without troubling your mind with how you will get there. The idea behind this affirmation practice is to firmly tell the universe what you want, without nitpicking the details about how you will get it, to allow many different paths for getting what you need as well as to manifest your desires more quickly.

Another way to use the Law of Attraction with visualization is to create a vision board. If you are a visual person, you may find this practice to be particularly helpful. For example, if you want to buy a house, start creating a collage of pictures of your ideal home even as you begin searching for it or applying for a loan. You can sift through magazines or the Internet for pictures of beautiful locations, amazing architecture, or welcoming interior design. Combine all of your ideas, hopes, and dreams into one large collage by cutting and gluing them in a single poster. You can keep your vision board on a special spiritual altar, or keep it where you will see it every day, like by your desk at work or even in your bathroom. The idea is for you to clearly visualize and manifest the existence of what you need on the astral plane and thus bring it into reality.

Vision boards can be created for almost anything, even to manifest an ideal lover. You can draw physical characteristics of a boyfriend or girlfriend of your dreams, or even add symbols such as wedding rings, hearts to show deep love, and other more personal reminders of the characteristics you are seeking in a life partner. You will still need to put yourself out there, since the perfect man or woman won't fall from the sky into your lap, but having a clear picture of what you need can at the very least speed up the process of recognition when you find it.

GROUNDING

Grounding, or the process of establishing a dynamic equilibrium of spiritual energy within your body, is another thing that everyone tends to do either consciously or unconsciously. Grounding is especially important before and after performing magic, when dealing with a stressful situation, or when facing interaction with a psychic vampire. It is my observation that most of the people I've met with bad luck tend to be chronically ungrounded, through no fault of their own. Even if the person can consciously perform grounding, he or she might be distracted by a terrible life event such as a divorce or a busy day at work. Or they might simply be subjected to an onslaught of energy-draining people, as is often the case with health workers and school teachers.

SYMPTOMS OF BAD LUCK
CAUSED BY CHRONIC LACK OF GROUNDING

Since the theory behind grounding is that healthy people always have a comfortable level of spiritual energy flowing through every cell in their bodies, an ungrounded person may have an excess of energy, or an energy deficit, or might have the related problem of stuck energy that requires spiritual cleansing. Since I am a very empathic person myself, I can easily experience terrible side effects if I do not keep myself grounded. One recent experience I had could have been easily interpreted as a curse if I had not recognized that I was in a situation of high spiritual energy.

I had traveled into a nearby city to attend a healing ritual that involved trance dancing. I enjoy trance dancing for the energy it can raise, but had never performed it with the particular group I was going to see that day. When I arrived at the building in which the dance was to happen, I was shocked to see how many people were in attendance. There was an

enormous dance space cleared out in the bottom floor basement area of an old structure where nearly a hundred strangers
began gathering in a circle to pray for healing and the release
of negative energy. The fact that negative energy was going to
be released by numerous people of varied life experience and
magical skill should have been my first warning.

Before we danced, I noticed how diverse the crowd was.
Many were college students from the nearby university, but
others were elderly, and quite a few appeared to be transients
from the street who had come in to escape the cold and their
troubles. Their faces faded from my attention as I began to
focus on my own movement and become lost in the music.
Long before the dance was to be finished, I began to feel
quite ill. My feet felt heavy, thumping the floor, and I was
nauseated and dizzy. I barely made it to sit on the floor at
the sidelines, stumbling as if I were drunk. I lay down on
the cool floor and noticed I was hot and sweaty despite having only danced slowly. I felt overcome with emotions that
weren't my own: anger, despair, and fear. I pressed my face
against the floor, not caring that it was dirty, and forcibly
grounded the energies that had clung to me. I left as quickly
as I could and never returned to a similar event. Those sorts
of intense situations just aren't right for me, and I am certain
I would manage to curse myself with lack of grounding if I
continued to tempt fate by attending.

If you have a build-up of energy that is blocked or imbal-
anced, the symptoms can be quite frightening and can easily
mimic those of a hex or even a possession. You might feel

jittery or paranoid. Your hands might shake. You may have sleepless nights or your sleep may be plagued with uncomfortably intense dreams. You might feel irritable or even have mood swings that seem inexplicable. Some people even report strange electrical phenomena, like radio static or lights and appliances turning on and off. Others may notice candle flames and other fire sources flaring up nearby, or objects falling off of shelves. Such symptoms can terrify you and cause the problem to get worse.

If you have a deficiency of energy, naturally a sense of lethargy and depression might result. You can feel like you are missing a sense of direction, or that time is passing incredibly slowly or, conversely, that the world is rushing by you too quickly. You may feel a sense of disconnection from your physical body, or a distortion of time and space. A lack of spiritual energy can easily feel like a curse. It can make the effects of any negativity in your life seem overwhelming, when under normal circumstances you would more easily bounce back.

Luckily, the solution for deficient or excess energy is the same as the one for negative energy: grounding to establish a connection with the earth and allowing your spiritual energy to reach equilibrium. Most people practice grounding with visualization, which I will describe, along with some helpful tips for those of you who are new to consciously grounding yourselves.

As a beginner, you may find it helpful to find a relaxing and quiet place to ground yourself so you can concentrate undisturbed. Outdoor places can be naturally very grounding, as can a cool, dark room. Removing your socks and shoes to create a physical connection to the ground can promote grounding. An alternative can be to hold a piece of hematite or other natural stone in your bare hand. Some people who have difficulty with visualization eat a heavy meal or place a bit of salt on the tongue to aid grounding, but ideally you won't have to use food as a crutch whenever you feel ungrounded.

Begin by attempting to perceive the energy in your body by closing your eyes and imagining that your body is a vessel in which a substance can move. You might see the energy in your mind's eye as a brightly colored light, a liquid, a smoke, or anything else that can move. Some people choose to imagine their entire body as a tree, or as filled with small creatures that represent energy. If you aren't the visual type, you might feel the energy as a soft fuzziness or a pressure, and that is okay as long as you can easily perceive its presence, absence, and movement.

Once you notice the energy in your body, try to become aware of your connection with the earth through your feet or the place where you are sitting. Even if you are in an airplane or a tall building, you can visualize a line of connection with the earth that is our home. Know that the earth is a well of energy if you feel deficient, and it is also a safe place to harmlessly disperse energy if you feel like you have an excess. Begin by pushing stale, stuck, or excess energy out of your body by visualizing or feeling the sensation of it flowing out of you. Then, draw refreshing new energy back up from the earth into your body. Even if you don't have excess energy, don't be afraid to push and pull from the earth as if you were breathing air in and out of your body.

It will take time and experience to feel when you have established the right equilibrium. Everyone is different, but generally you should feel calm yet alert when the process has been successfully completed. Grounding can be performed whenever your mind turns to bad luck, and it can also be done regularly throughout the day, such as when you wake up, at lunch time, and when you go to bed, in order to stave off bad luck blights.

MEDITATION

Meditation is a practice known to reduce stress, lower blood pressure, and provide other health benefits to the body. Meditation can also eliminate runs of bad luck by bringing your mind, body, and spirit into the moment, to stop the bad habit the mind has of focusing on negative past experiences or dreading the future. Meditation can take many forms, some of which include movement, visualization, or receiving messages from spirits or other entities.

The spiritual style of meditation I recommend for warding off bad luck is different from the receptive trance state I recommend for psychic work. Instead of attempting to perceive external cues, the goal of meditation for health and good luck should be to connect you with the moment, your true life's purpose, and with your higher power if you believe in one. Some call the latter form of meditation transmission meditation, because it allows positive energy to be transmitted from the universe (and perhaps a higher power) through you and out into your life and your world. In addition to helping your life, transmission meditation can be thought of as an act of service, since it improves your outlook and thus your influence on the globe.

Step 1.) Set up the space. All meditation should ideally be performed in a relaxing environment with few distractions. As a beginner, you may find it helpful to be in a completely silent and dimly lit room, seated in a comfortable but upright position. As you gain experience, you may be able to transition to meditation in a variety of settings, but it can be frustrating as a beginner to find yourself unable to concentrate because of your surroundings. Make sure that the doors are locked and your phone ringers are turned off, so that you won't be disturbed. I find that it helps to set a timer so that I won't be peeking at the clock to see how long I have meditated. Those experienced with transmission meditation can perform it daily for two hours or more, but I suggest not pushing yourself. A reasonable goal for the enthusiastic beginner is ten minutes, moving to twenty and then thirty. If you are especially distractible, as I am, don't be ashamed to start at five minutes or even less.

Step 2.) The invocation. An invocation is a special type of prayer in which a higher power, or your goal of having good luck, is drawn down into your soul so that you can hold it mindfully during meditation. There are invocations used in transmission meditation in many different languages, and you can feel free to create your own, but I suggest that you memorize and use the same one for your daily or frequent practice, so that you won't be straining to invent a new prayer each time and can more easily fall into a relaxed meditation.

If you are new to prayer, or feel awkward about it due to your relationship with faith, you may feel very awkward at first. You might even wish to have a little talk with the deity or deities to whom you are praying first, and introduce yourself by name. I suggest praying in private so that any sense of inhibition in front of other people will be eliminated. I'll include a prayer template here for those of you who may be unfamiliar with the practice. I like to use the mnemonic of the letters in the word PRAYING for this formula: Person listening, Raise praise, Ask for help, Your deadline, Imperatives for safety, Note of thanks, and Gracious attention.

PERSON LISTENING
I invoke [God(s)/Goddess(es)/Spirit/
Universe/my Higher Self/etc.]

RAISE PRAISE
You who is/are the source of all good luck,
love, and light, deserving of my praise!

ASK FOR HELP
*Thank you for allowing your good luck to stream
down into me to guide my will and purpose,
and to put all bad luck harmlessly in its place.*

YOUR DEADLINE
Now.

IMPERATIVES FOR SAFETY
*With harm to none, and for the
highest good of all. So may it be.*

NOTE OF THANKS
In return, I offer you my service to our world.

GRACIOUS ATTENTION
*Blessed be. (Meditate and then reflect
on how you felt during and after.)*

Step 3.) Meditation time. For the duration of time that you
have chosen, close your eyes and attempt to clear your
mind by focusing your attention on a point on your forehead between your eyes. The energy center on your forehead is thought to be a place where energy from a higher
power can flow directly into your soul, and keeping your
attention high during meditation can prevent distraction
as well as keep the purpose of your meditation focused on
transmitting good luck instead of receiving psychic messages or slipping into another form of meditation.

Step 4.) Keep your concentration, which is easier said than done. You may easily find your thoughts drifting away to work, bills, or what you're going to have for dinner. You might also find your attention shifting down to your solar plexus, especially if you are used to meditating with a focus there for psychic work. In your mind, cue yourself to clear your mind and bring your attention back to the middle of your forehead. Some choose to imagine or say the word *aum* or *om*, which reflects all possible vowel sounds, symbolically representing the entirety of the universe. As you become experienced, you may find you need to inwardly sound a cue less often, but my husband just started meditating and he says he has to sound the "om" with each breath.

Step 5.) When your time is up—and hopefully you have a relatively peaceful-sounding timer go off—take a moment to sit receptively and reflect on your feelings. Some people see lights and hear sounds during or directly after meditation, while others have major life revelations in the moments or days following a good meditation session. You may choose to journal your thoughts during this time. It is good to ground yourself after meditation, especially if you're just starting your day and are about to go to work. It is not always necessary to ground yourself before meditation, unless you find yourself falling asleep or feeling too wired to relax.

I'll be the first to admit that meditation of any kind is just plain hard for some people. It was and still is difficult for me, so I have to treat it like any other exercise or chore. And just as one might make plans to attend a class or take a friend to the gym for some accountability, I've started inviting friends over to my home to meditate with me so I won't just skip this important aspect of self-care. If you find meditation challenging, try not to ruminate about how hard it is in the moment, and instead watch for changes that happen in the rest of your life as a result of starting a regular meditation practice. Watching your bad luck melt away and seeing other health benefits pop up can be just the motivation you need to stick with it.

How to talk to a loved one who is imagining a case of black magic

I'm sure that the above solutions may have inspired some of you who suffer from bad luck. However, what about the heartbreaking case in which a friend, parent, or other loved one has been deceived or confused into believing in a curse? Frustratingly enough, it never seems to be those gullible, dense types you can just smack on the back of the head and yell "knock it off!" Often the most deeply deluded are intelligent people you respect. You feel that you could lose a friendship or invoke a great deal of ire if you try to tell this person he or she is wrong.

First, you should put the situation into context. Is your loved one's culture of origin filled with hexes and curses, and is this something that he or she has battled for an entire lifetime? Or is this newfound fear of a curse borne from a scary movie that was viewed last week and will blow over in time? Either of these situations may not warrant an over-reaction on your part. If hexes are a culture concept with which your loved one is familiar, he or she may already have a solution or plan of action, even if the hex isn't real, that will be harmless at worst. Allow your loved one to receive an extraneous exorcism or to go through any other rites or prayers he or she feels are appropriate, even if you're quite sure that a hex exists. Likewise, if your loved one is just the type that spooks easily, and a hex is something new and random in a long line of unreasonable fears, you might just freak him or her out more if you start throwing out spooky ritual ideas or suggest that there might be a mental illness at work. Instead, offer your love and empathy for the genuine feelings of fear, and wait for the phase to pass.

The only time that you should intervene in a loved one's life if an imagined hex is at work is if his or her life is being severely adversely affected by the belief. For example, if your grandparent is shelling out thousands of dollars to a phony psychic to perform a hex removal, it is time to step in. If your sister is so freaked out by a fear of a curse that she won't even leave her house to go to work, she needs help.

The best thing you can do for a loved one who is difficult to confront is to respectfully find resources and reinforce-ments. I don't mean to tell his or her friends, family, and the world. Embarrassing your loved one will only make the situ-ation worse. Instead, appeal to a more confidential author-ity. For instance, you might want to contact a professional therapist to act as a mediator between the two of you, or you could approach a clergy member at your loved one's place of worship to ask for spiritual counseling.

It may sound hokey, but try to use "I" statements that keep the focus on your concerns and your needs without sounding accusatory. Start out by telling him or her how you feel and then offering a suggestion for how he or she can help you. For example, you might say, "Mom, I've been feeling anxious and sad that you won't fly in an airplane to come see me because you believe that you have a curse on you. Will you please help me enjoy your company once again by seeking help from your pastor to talk about your fears?"

In the above example, the focus is kept on you and your concerns and problems, which helps the person to avoid becoming defensive about his or her own problems. If, instead, you had pointed out "you're being sucked in by a scam" or "your beliefs are wrong and crazy," your worries would likely be dismissed. Worse still, your loved one might begin hiding certain behaviors like giving money to hex-removal specialists. Or they may become more and more isolated due to fears of driving or being around other people while in a hexed state.

As a last resort, if a loved one will not listen to reason and you feel that he or she is gravely disabled by believing in a curse, you can go directly to the proper authorities. If a scammer is the culprit for the erroneous hex belief, you can call the police to investigate and provide as much proof as possible about the monetary transactions and hex claims.

If your loved one is beginning to have failing health, or is unable to work or have relationships due to hex fears, you can contact your local emergency services to have his or her mental health evaluated by medical professionals.

It is heartbreaking to have to betray a loved one's wishes by turning to authority figures. Leave it as a last resort, since those feelings you have that your loved one will never want to speak to you again are legitimate. But if his or her financial livelihood or health is at stake, remember that you might be thanked later. At the very least, an intervention may be worth it to save somebody from living with unnecessary fear.

The special case in which a loved one thinks her new baby is possessed or hexed

Some physiological processes have taken on their own mythology throughout human history. The experience of sleep apnea was once commonly thought to be caused by demons attacking victims as they slept. Similarly, many cultures have the perception that some newborn babies are switched at birth by fairies, born without a soul, or possessed by some evil entity. The real culprit behind these feelings may be serious hormonal disorders such as postpartum depression and postpartum psychosis. As the hormone levels change immediately after pregnancy, perfectly sane women can experience hallucinations, delusions, and even thoughts of harming or killing themselves or their babies.

If a loved one you know believes her newborn to be cursed or possessed, call for help from the police or emergency medical personnel right away if she won't go to the hospital for help. Even the most loving mothers can and do hurt themselves and their babies when suffering from postpartum depression or psychosis, so the problem must be handled immediately through medical means before providing any spiritual solutions for any long-term feelings about the baby. Once the disease in the mother is managed, most likely any feelings about hexes or possession in the infant will disappear without the need for a hex removal.

FOUR

———— ✕•◎•✕ ————

How to break a curse

Let's say that your logical deduction and psychic divination have led to the same conclusion—that a hex has been placed upon you or a loved one. It can be exhilarating to finally feel certainty about your experience, but also terrifying if you are inexperienced with magic, especially if you have had others tell you that hex removal is costly or difficult. Luckily, there are as many ways to remove a hex as there are ways to place a hex, as people have been working throughout time to counteract the forces of magic as quickly as they have been advancing magical knowledge, in a sort of magical arms race. In order to reduce confusion, I will begin with the easiest and most effective techniques that can be used on many types of hexes.

How do hexes end on their own?

Before we jump into hex removal, it may be useful for you to know how hexes run their course if nobody interferes with them. The duration of a hex has to do with the manner in which the spell was cast and the experience of the person performing the magic.

Some magical practitioners use energy flowing through their own bodies to charge a hex or an object associated with a hex. In that case, the hex may slowly peter out as the practitioner is unable to uphold continued focus on the hex over time. With this kind of practice, the hex would definitely end with the death of the practitioner. If you already know who your enemy is, you will be able to detect this kind of hex if you see the effects diminish when your enemy is distracted with other things in life. Hex prevention, which is covered later in this book, would in this case involve trying to work things out with your enemy.

If the hex is associated with an object or specific props, the destruction or decay of the enchanted objects can break the hex. This is because the objects have been charged with the energy powering the hex. When the objects are destroyed, the energy is dispersed, hopefully harmlessly into the earth. If you have an object that you want to destroy safely in order to rid it of a hex, read the following section on removing curses from objects.

Many practitioners create a hex for a specific outcome, such as a lover breaking up with his or her beloved. Sometimes a hex can be cleverly broken by figuring out what outcome the practitioner desired, and then temporarily creating those conditions. For example, if a hex was placed on a couple to divorce them, divorce papers could be signed, and then the couple immediately remarried, and the hex would be broken even if they had never actually wanted to be parted from one another.

What if you're unlucky enough to have an experienced magical practitioner who knows how to incorporate timing working against you? Many systems of magic include the use of timing. It not only aids the spell's force, but also sets a start date for the peak effects and an end date for when the hex should be over. Timing is very important for magic. For example, a person planning a hurtful hex might choose to perform the hex during a waning moon to represent decay, and on a Tuesday, the day associated with destruction. A skilled practitioner will set a specific time for the hex to manifest itself, since he or she wants to hurt you, and it's probably not satisfying to watch you live to a ripe old age and *then* break a hip. So a common caveat will be added for the effects to be seen by the next full moon, when you will notice the peak effects of the curse. After that, if the outcome has occurred, the hex will naturally end unless your enemy casts another spell or asks for the curse to continue until an end date. Unfortunately, the end date can vary, since you will have no idea if he or she designed the curse to end in three weeks, three months, or any other arbitrary length of time.

If you are quite certain that you have been hexed, it is a good idea to remove the hex rather than to figure out when it will end on its own, since you may have no idea if your hex is set simply on a specific outcome, or has an end date in the distant future. If the hex is placed directly on a person, a speedy hex removal is of great importance. If you believe that the easy and quick methods of hex removal appearing here seem *too* easy, you're welcome to try more advanced spiritual cleansing or banishing rituals afterward. If things progress to that level, please start from the most minimal intervention so you can have the best chance of stopping the effects of the curse quickly, before they progress.

How to remove a hex from yourself, all by yourself, for free

The most simple, quick, and effective way to remove any curse is through prayer. Of course, this may seem like a confounding paradox to someone who is an atheist or presently experiencing a crisis of faith. But since prayer is so effective for so many, it deserves a try before any other hex removal tactic. If you are an atheist, you may feel uncomfortable directing a prayer to a source of divinity, but you can think of your prayer as going to your higher self or the deep subconscious archetype of power you have over your own life and destiny. In times of curse or strife, many people feel comfortable going back to the prayers and deities honored in their childhood, since that was a source of comfort in the past, and those with newly discovered faith may find instant renewal through their newfound relationship with a higher power. It is perfectly okay to do both; there's no such thing as prayer overkill.

Remember the PRAYING mnemonic I taught earlier for prayer: Person listening, Raise praise, Ask for help, Your deadline, Imperatives for safety, Note of thanks, and Gracious attention. I'll give another example of the format below for a hex removal, and then later in this chapter I'll refer back to this prayer format with some suggestions for changing it to make the prayer more appropriate for the need.

PERSON LISTENING
Hail, [God(s)/Goddess(es)/Spirit/
Universe/Higher Self/etc.]

RAISE PRAISE
You who is/are [list three positive
attributes], I praise you!

ASK FOR HELP
Thank you for removing any hex
or negative energy from me.

YOUR DEADLINE
Now.

IMPERATIVES FOR SAFETY
With harm to none, and for the
highest good of all. So may it be.

NOTE OF THANKS
*In return, I offer you [gratitude/
love and devotion/other offering].*

GRACIOUS ATTENTION
Blessed be.

*Pause, take three deep breaths, and be silent
and alert for a sign, an answer, or any other
physical sensation or mental feeling.*

Prayer is ideally a two-way communication with deity, the universe, or your higher self, and it can be especially important to sit receptively after praying for a hex removal. Since your own emotional state of mind can affect the course of a hex and can affect your life even without the presence of a hex—as will be discussed later—experiencing a sense of relief or freedom immediately after prayer can help carry you to a more positive life ahead. You do not need to repeat the prayer for the same hex, just trust that it will be removed and allow yourself to move forward psychologically from this bump in your life. You should notice the effects of a prayer immediately and completely.

If you do not feel a sense of salvation from prayer, don't despair. You can check again to see if the effects of the curse are gone. If you feel like the prayer didn't work, there is nothing wrong with you. Conflict about spirituality and religious turmoil are not new human conditions, and are perfectly reasonable reactions to having suffered a hex or any other life challenge. Feelings of anger with God or faltering faith are why most hospitals have a spiritual care department filled with chaplains to counsel patients, families, and health care providers during transformative life experiences. If prayer isn't meeting your expectations right now, you aren't a failure, it doesn't mean there is no God, and it doesn't mean you should give up. Continue to work on praying as much as you are comfortable, but feel free to read onward about spiritual cleansing and banishing rituals that may feel more spiritually nourishing for you during this time. There is a special circumstance that can occur in either yourself or another person called possession, which means that the hex takes the form of a magical entity. The cure for possession is exorcism, which will be discussed later in this chapter.

You can also ask for a person of faith such as a friend or relative, or a spiritual leader at your place of worship, to pray for you. The prayer above, or others like it, will work even if prayed for you by another person at a distance. Again, you should still be wary of any professional who demands money in exchange for prayer. Although some faith traditions such as Vodou may have clergy and spiritual practices that indicate monetary exchange for prayer, there are always free resources to receive prayer if you don't have the means or inclination to pay.

How to remove a hex from another person

As has already been mentioned, prayer can be said for another person in order to remove a hex. However, prayer, or any other form of hex removal for that matter, should be done only with permission. So if you know a loved one who has the capacity to give his or her consent and is suffering from a hex, please ask for that consent before performing any hex removal, and respect his or her response. If you push onward and force a hex removal on a person against his or her will, your well-meaning attempt may backfire and amplify the effects of the hex. Everyone has the natural ability to strongly resist energy that is being aimed in his or her general direction, and if you inspire somebody to deflect your positive energy, the remaining negative energy can be concentrated in his or her life. Not only that, but once your loved one's defenses are raised, he or she may block positive energies from other sources that would have otherwise been lovingly accepted. Praying for somebody in secret may seem like a good idea, but it can be disrespectful to deities in some faith traditions. An especially sensitive loved one may be able to detect the effects of an unwanted prayer, even if performed in secret. Besides, telling somebody that you are praying for them shows that you care, which can enhance their emotional health and give them spiritual fortitude.

Why would somebody refuse a hex removal? The most likely reason would be a denial that a hex exists in the first place. If that is the case, you don't have to badger somebody into admitting something is true when they have no basis for belief. Instead, you can express positive wishes that you have for that person's life that he or she can get behind, along with a potential solution. For example, you can say, "Dad, I would love for you to be healthier. Is it okay if I pray for you?" Another objection to hex removal can be offense taken at a different faith tradition. You may wish to offer other resources to your loved one. For example, "Sister, it pains me that you have been struggling so much with your love life recently. Is it okay if I ask the pastor at your church to say a prayer for you anonymously?" If your loved one is steadfastly against prayer, you may find other solutions that are more to his or her liking, such as rituals or making a talisman, as described in chapter 6, for hex prevention.

Once you've obtained permission from your loved one to perform a hex removal, you can adapt the prayer above, or one like it, in order to perform the removal. Unless you are comfortable praying to your loved one's higher power, if it differs from your own, you should address your own higher power when praying for another. However, if it is in your comfort zone to pray to a different deity that your loved one honors, please do so, as the extra positive effect of your loved one's relationship with that spiritual source of power will boost the effect of the prayer.

Again, use the prayer format given above if you are comfortable with it. Of course, you'll have to insert the name of the person for whom you are asking help.

ASK FOR HELP
*Thank you for removing any hex
or negative energy from [full name].*

During the Gracious attention phase, pause first to listen to your higher self for any feedback about the prayer. Then tell the person for whom you have prayed to close his or her eyes, take three deep breaths, and tell you how they feel. Hopefully your loved one will feel a sense of reverence and relief. You can also take time afterward for divination to verify that the hex has been removed, if you have any doubts.

How to remove a family
curse or a hex on a group

Sometimes curses are placed on entire groups of people. Cursed groups can be anything from a couple or small family unit to an entire family line, tribe, or worship group. While in modern Western culture it is very unlikely for one's knitting club or sports team to be cursed, in some cultures, curses are cast upon everyone who is perceived to be in an enemy group. If all of the group members are living and in one place, it can be simple enough to gather all the affected victims together and have them share a prayer or be prayed over by one person in order to remove the curse, as in the prayer instructions above for a single person. However, it is not practical to be able to gather every member of an entire group in some instances, or some of the affected members may no longer be living. Ideally, the curse should be lifted from both the living and nonliving members of the group. This removes any possible effects from the dead, such as potentially being bound in ghost form or, if one believes in reincarnation, experiencing curse effects when reborn into a new body. More importantly, because the curse was cast on the entire group, it should be removed from the entire group.

Lifting a curse the same way it was placed

As a brief aside, I'd like to explain why you should lift a curse in the same way it was placed, since it applies to removing a curse from an entire group of people even if you only care about one person that the curse has affected. In Western magical practice, all spells and rituals are initiated and ended in a similar way. All of the ritual tools and mental constructs are set up before a spell and then carefully taken down in reverse order, without missing anything that was placed. Due to the magical Law of Association, casting a spell is a lot like weaving a complicated tapestry. All of the elements of the ritual and spell hang together just so, and in order to dismantle the spell completely, it is best to unravel all that has been done, since trying to tear it up may leave complete pieces intact that can have unpredictable results.

Ideally, this means that you could perform a reverse ritual that was very similar to the original hex ritual in order to completely annul it. However, very rarely will your enemy reveal all of the details of what he or she has done, so you'll have to resort to more general methods. Think of prayer as a broad-spectrum antibiotic to treat a disease. The more detailed I get with the rituals below, the more I am tailoring the hex removal to the problem at hand, much like a doctor might choose a specific antibiotic if the exact bacterial infection was known.

Using a symbol to represent a group

So if you have an entire cursed race of people, and you can't possibly gather all affected people together for prayer due to moral objections from some of them, members being deceased, or even not knowing all of the people who are affected, you will have to start getting symbolic with your magic. Create a symbol to represent the affected group. In some cases this may be obvious, such as a family crest, or if your sports team really was cursed, your team mascot. Additionally, there are also ways you can make special magical symbols called sigils for anything.

A sigil is a magical symbol that is created to condense an idea into a visual symbol that can be used in a spell. One of the easiest ways to make sigils that are very powerful is to overlap the letters of a word right on top of one another, so that they may share some lines. For example, the name Bob could be written so that it was just a B with an O encircling it. Anyone else looking at the sigil would only see a letter B and a circle, but the person who made the circle could look at the letter B as two. The letter in the name Ed would share a vertical line. As you can see, the more letters you use, the more obscure the sigil may look to anyone who was not involved in its creation.

Colors of the sigil are also important, both for the material on which the sigil is written, and the ink used to inscribe the sigil. Since you are making a sigil for a group, think of not only an appropriate name for the group, but also two colors that represent it. If colors simply don't apply to your group for whatever reason, you can also use a white background to represent the deflection of negative energy and a blue pen to represent healing, since white paper and blue pens are also easily available in a pinch.

When you create your sigil, gather an appropriately colored pen with water-soluble ink and a piece of paper. Ground yourself first. You may wish to set up some psychic shielding as described in the chapter on preventing a hex, especially if you are part of the accursed group, or if you feel that you may be in danger of being hexed for playing a role in the hex's removal. Concentrate on the group of people you wish to represent with the sigil, and picture as many of the members as you can clearly in your mind's eye. Inscribe the sigil on your piece of paper. Now that you have a sigil, you can pray over it as you would a person, and you can use the instructions for removing a hex from an object as given below.

How to remove a hex from an object

Several clients have sent me objects they believe to be cursed in order to have the curses removed (for free). Most often these objects are jewelry. In a couple of cases, the objects were rings given by former lovers. In one case, the object was a locket given to a child victim, who experienced hair loss until the curse was removed from the object. In all cases, these jewelry pieces were given to me so I could remove the curses permanently, but they were not returned to the owners due to the curse removal process.

For the child, the mother contacted me and told me a terrible story of a nasty divorce, in which her former husband had placed a curse on her daughter from a previous marriage. Her daughter, still young, was experiencing rapid hair loss after having been given a cursed locket by the ex-husband, and doctors couldn't explain what caused it. I first made sure that the mother had taken her daughter to medical professionals to make sure there was no underlying illness. I asked for no money to remove the curse from her daughter, but I did have to take the locket in order to destroy it. The mother had already sent it away to somebody else through the mail for safekeeping, which I don't recommend for a hexed object. You wouldn't want to accidentally affect a mail carrier. When it was returned to her, she gave it to me, and I destroyed it during the curse removal process after verifying that the object had been cursed. The daughter's hair grew back after the curse was removed from the locket, and I didn't have to remove any curse from the daughter directly. Since the curse was cast through the locket, it was possible to remove it in its destruction.

Placing a curse on an object is a common method of hexing a target. The reason for this is because several laws of magic can be easily put into play when creating the hexed object, including the Laws of Association and Contagion, and an attractive object can easily deliver a hex to a person who might otherwise be on his or her guard from contact with an enemy.

Unfortunately, the Law of Contagion often makes cursed objects very effective because even if the object is thrown away, the effects of the curse will still continue to plague the person who touched it. The best way to end the curse is by removing it from the object.

As explained earlier in this chapter, the most effective way to get rid of a curse would be to carefully unravel it in the same way it was created. For a hexed object, this means that the best course of action would be to destroy the object, if it is practical. You might recall the central myth of *The Lord of the Rings,* in which a cursed ring had to be destroyed in the same fires in which it was created. However, destroying the object must be done carefully so that unwanted effects do not happen to people when the curse is released from the object. For that reason, you may have to temporarily store the object before you get a chance to remove the curse. To store a cursed object safely, pack it in salt in a box or sealed bag and place it somewhere safe where nobody will touch it, preferably buried in the earth.

When you get to a time and place in which you can remove the curse from the object, you can start by protecting yourself with psychic shielding or a magic circle as described in the section on preventing hexes. To destroy the object, you won't be literally dismantling it in the exact same way that it was made, but symbolically you will reduce it to its component parts. In magic, the symbolic puzzle pieces that put the entire universe together are the four elements of earth, air, fire, and water. Ancient magicians believed that everything was made up of a combination of one or more of those four elements, so they are still used today to divide up and categorize things in the universe and in magic.

Destroying a cursed object with fire

Fire is by far the most commonly used element to destroy a cursed object because it is so effective at reducing it to ashes. To destroy an object with fire, first make sure that you're not going to hurt anyone physically in the process; use a safe area with adequate ventilation. It is okay to use firewood, paper, and other fuels to get the fire going and to keep it burning until the object is completely burned. After setting up your psychic protection but before saying your prayer over the object, build your fire. If the object is made of metal or another material that is difficult to burn, you may have to build a very big fire and burn it for quite some time so as to generate hot coals that can melt metal or glass.

When the fire is ready, say the prayer, similar to the one in the prayer section above, replacing the person's name with the object's name, or the group's name if you are using a sigil to represent a group of people. If you have a physical offering to your higher power(s) such as incense, you can burn the offering right after burning the accursed object. Place special emphasis on your words asking for no harm to come from the destruction of the object. As you watch the object's destruction in the fire, visualize in your mind's eye the energy flowing harmlessly into the earth below and dispersing so as to become invisible and ineffective. You might "see" the hex energy as a black liquid or smoke.

Use the hex removal format again, this time using the name of the object or group. I also like to give special concentration and emphasis to the "with harm to none and for the highest good of all" line to underscore the importance of giving only blessings to all concerned.

ASK FOR HELP
Thank you for removing any hex or
negative energy from [object/group].

IMPERATIVES FOR SAFETY
With harm to none, and for the
highest good of all. So may it be.

When you are quite sure that the object has been destroyed, you can extinguish the fire safely or let it burn down. Collect the ashes from the destroyed object. You can scatter these ashes to wind or flowing water, but I recommend burying the ashes under a living plant. The plant can indicate to you the effectiveness of the curse removal by continuing its healthy growth. Of course, plants have lifespans like anything else, but in the highly unlikely case that the plant withers or dies overnight, it can be an indication that the ritual needs to be repeated with the ashes, or that you may wish to look into the other rituals included in this chapter. A repeat is likely only to be needed if the object survived the fire relatively intact.

Destroying a cursed object with air

Since air isn't an incredibly destructive force except in storms, the way to invite the element of air into your ritual is by scattering ashes from a fire ritual to the wind, or by adding incense to a fire ritual. Using air to destroy an object isn't necessary, and is not usually the most practical, but I include it here for the sake of completion, and in case you have nowhere to bury ashes.

Destroying a cursed object with water

In addition to disposing of ashes in running water, such as a river or stream, I've asked you to make sigils on paper with water-soluble ink for a reason. Using filter paper may also aid in the following working. A powerful spell tactic, used as far back as ancient Egypt, employs the dissolving of ink in water. Gather your tools, including your sigil and a bowl of water. It is okay to make the sigil during the same ritual, if you haven't already. Protect yourself with psychic shielding or a magic circle. Say a prayer to remove the hex, and dip the sigil in the water to allow the ink to dissolve as much as possible. As you dissolve the ink, again visualize the hex energy dripping down through the bowl into the earth and dispersing harmlessly. The paper doesn't need to be destroyed completely, but if it does tear or begin to disintegrate in the process, that's okay.

After the ink has dissolved from the paper, bury the remaining paper under a living plant and water it with the inky water byproduct. Again, the condition of the plant immediately after disposing of the object can give you a good indication of whether the curse has been removed completely. Nontoxic water-soluble ink should not harm the plant.

Destroying a cursed object with earth

At the end of each of the previous elemental destructions, I advise burying the remains of the object in earth. Indeed, many cultures skip all other steps entirely and bury cursed objects to allow natural weathering processes to destroy them. I do not find immediate burial to be preferable because the destruction may take a considerable length of time, during which the curse's effects may still be felt. However, some may choose to use earth to destroy a curse if they don't wish to handle the cursed object long enough to destroy it with fire, or if they choose to take a longer destruction method for sentimental reasons, such as to get rid of an engagement or wedding ring.

To destroy an object in earth, I recommend packing it first with salt and wrapping it with filter paper. This will allow the curse-blocking magical purification properties of the salt to deaden hex effects as well as allow the salt to corrode the object if possible. Because of the salt and the intact object, please do not bury the cursed object under a live plant if trying to destroy it with earth. The salt and any chemicals leaching from the object can kill the plant regardless of the curse.

Since destruction of an object through natural earth processes takes time anyway, you may wish to use the best magical timing possible. The ideal time to bury a cursed object would be at night, during a waning moon, to allow the moon's waning energy to take away the curse effects. If possible, winter is the best burial time, but that may not be practical if you live in an area where the ground freezes in winter. If ideal circumstances are not available to you, bury the object whenever you can. Use psychic protection or a magic circle and say a prayer before dropping the object in a hole and covering it. It is important to undertake the burial in secrecy and on your own private land so that a curious person does not dig up the cursed object. After burying the object, pour a pitcher of water over the burial site in offering to the source of your answered prayers, and also to aid decay or corrosion of the object. Take a moment to visualize the negative energy of the curse washing off the object, dripping into the earth and dispersing harmlessly.

What if you want to preserve the object?

In some cases, you may not want to destroy the accursed object. Perhaps the cursed object is valuable jewelry that you want to sell, or maybe it has sentimental value and you wish to use the object safely. Depending on the way that the person who hexed your object performed the spell, it may be possible to remove the hex from the object safely and still use it afterward using a modified earth burial procedure, similar to the earth destruction listed above.

To deaden the curse effects, you'll still want to pack the object in salt. But to protect the object from actually being destroyed by the salt, particularly if it is made of a metal that can be corroded, I suggest this time sealing the object first in a plastic baggie, then sealing the smaller plastic baggie inside a larger salt-filled baggie so it is completely surrounded by the salt. Packed this way, the salt doesn't actually touch the object and also won't leach into the earth. The reason you don't want the salt to leach out into the earth this time is to keep the salt in close proximity to the accursed object for as long as possible, so that the working will have maximum effect.

Decide where you want to bury the object. Of course, it will need to be done in a private place on your own property so that no curious person will suffer negative effects by digging up the object before the curse has been fully removed. Since the salt and object will be sealed in a baggie, you may bury it next to a living plant. This will yield two added benefits: the plant will serve as a marker so you can find it, and the health of the plant will verify whether or not the curse is still effective, even before you have dug up the object.

Bury the object during a waning moon, and if possible and practical, during the winter. You will be leaving the object buried for at least one full moon cycle. I suggest digging it up during a waxing or full moon, which would mean you leave it buried until the moon wanes completely to dark, waxes completely until full, and then wanes completely until dark. Then when the moon waxes toward full again, you may dig up the item and test to see if it has been freed. If you have the patience and the ability to bury it during winter, I suggest digging it up the following spring during a waxing or full moon. The winter season and the waning energy of the moon can help the curse fade and decay, while the waxing or full moon in spring can help imbue the object with renewed, positive energy when it is once again liberated from the salt and earth. Be sure to add the time frame you have chosen to your prayer when burying the object.

Using the PRAYING format already given, there are two lines that need a bit of alteration to make them more appropriate.

ASK FOR HELP
Thank you for removing any hex or negative energy from this [object].

YOUR DEADLINE
Now. Let the [object] be safe for use by the next [spring/full moon/etc.].

As with the more destructive version of earth hex removal, pour a pitcher of water over the place where the object has been buried after you fill in the hole, and visualize the negative energy being washed off of the object and being dispersed into the surrounding soil and earth in a harmless way. When you dig up the object, the curse should be gone as indicated by the state of the plant near which it was buried. If you wish, you may perform divination to verify that the curse is gone. No further magic needs performing, and no more words need to be said about the matter unless you choose to bless or protect the object from future hexes (chapter 6 has more information).

There is a special circumstance in which an object can become a home for a magical entity, in which case the object is called a "fetter." Fetters and the cure for the fetter, called an exorcism, will be covered later in this chapter.

How to remove a curse from a place

The cursing of a place most commonly happens for one of three reasons. Either the place is important to the person who cast the curse and the hex was placed for a protective reason, the place became naturally cursed through a traumatic or negative magical event taking place there, or it became cursed due of a magical entity residing there. Although people can be possessed and objects can become fetters, places are the most likely way to find magical entities "in the wild" that have not been placed there purposely by another person. Please read the section later in this chapter about banishing rituals, which are used to cure a place haunted by any sort of magical entity.

If the place has been cursed by a person, look around for objects or markings that have been left behind in the process of a curse. If the place is a house with a hearth or fire pit, look for evidence there. Look also at the threshold of entry into the place, be it a door or a pathway. It is also possible for evidence to be left on the floor or ceiling. Evidence of a curse may be an object left behind, such as the remains of a dead animal or insect; a human-shaped doll, figure, or picture; colored string, cloth, or paper; or a small bag of objects. If you find some-thing suspicious in the cursed place, perform divination to check and see whether the object is cursed, and if it is, you can follow instructions to dispose of the object as found earlier in this chapter.

Markings may be left in paint, chalk, pencil, or ink that look like symbols such as an X, a sigil, or a picture of a person or an animal that has been harmed or bound. It is not enough to simply paint over a magical mark, because the effects will persist. Instead, clean off the marking in whatever way you can, and then scrub the area with salt water while saying a prayer. Remove the curse as if the wall, floor or whatever else has been marked, is also a cursed object.

Once any markings or objects present have been dealt with separately, you may pray to remove a hex from the place. Make sure to psychically shield yourself before the prayer, and I highly recommend looking forward to chapter 6 to learn how to cast a magic circle around the entire place. After you have removed the hex, you may wish to bless the place, using information provided in the chapter on hex prevention. Note that simple hex removal is not appropriate when the place isn't actually cursed by a magical practitioner but is instead inhabited by a malevolent entity or is harboring negative energy from something that occurred at that location. Read onward in the following sections about banishing rituals and cleansing rituals in those circumstances. However, for a straightforward hex removal, the usual prayer format will do, applying the prayer to a place and making sure to speak a deadline. Again, I like to place special emphasis on harming none if it is a public place.

ASK FOR HELP
Thank you for removing any hex or
negative energy from this [place].

YOUR DEADLINE
Now. Let the [place] be safe for use
by the next [spring/full moon/etc.].

IMPERATIVES FOR SAFETY
With harm to none, and for the
highest good of all. So may it be.

How to remove a hex that has been placed on a situation or event

Some hexes may be tricky because, instead of casting a spell upon a person, a magical practitioner may cast the spell on a specific life event. Some events that may be more likely to be cursed than others are one's sleeping hours or dreams, a wedding or the marriage itself, the birth of a child, or a person's promotion or rise to a place of authority or power.

In many cultures, classic tricks are used to avert the curse, such as using a fake baby to divert malevolent attention from the real baby. Or they will use a fake bride, or even annul a marriage and then renew vows later to create the circumstances required for the curse to run its course. Likewise, there are many hex prevention measures that are taken in such cultures surrounding important events such as these.

Although hex prevention for events may be important to you, depending on your culture and enemies, if you believe that a hex has already been cast, I recommend using the sigil method described above in the section on a curse affecting a whole group of people. Create a sigil that represents the event or situation that has been cursed, and then destroy the sigil using a hex removal method for objects.

How to make sure
the curse is gone for good

Before moving on with your life, you may feel nervous about the efficacy of your curse removal attempts. Since doubt and fear can have their own negative effects that might cause you to believe in a curse that doesn't exist, it is best to find ways to reassure yourself immediately if you feel any sense that the curse might remain. First, always make sure you add a time frame to your prayers for the curse to be gone, be it immediately, by the next full moon, next spring, or a date of your choosing. Never assume a curse is gone before your time frame is complete.

Many of the curse removal strategies for objects listed previously have the technique built in to bury the object beneath a plant and to observe the health of the plant as evidence of the absence of a curse. Using plants as curse indicators works well with objects that have been deliberately cursed because they can remain in close proximity to the plant for a time, and because the nature of a cursed object is to bring harm to what touches or surrounds it based on the magical Law of Contagion. For this reason, plants may also work as indicators in some cursed places, but won't work as indicators for cursed people who are being directly maligned or in places that have become home to malicious elementals, since the elementals may be friendlier toward plants than intruding people.

Performing divination again after a hex removal, banishing, or exorcism is a good way to see instant results. Return to chapter 2 for instructions on pertinent divination techniques to determine whether a hex is present If you had the foresight to perform divination ahead of time, you can directly compare the results to see an improvement, which can make the answer more certain since differences are easier to spot. Once you have your answer by divination, there is no need to keep checking up on the hex because it is gone. There is no hex that automatically renews itself on its own, because hexes require the energy of their maker to be created. Any future hexing situation should be dealt with as a separate incident. Repeat hex removals, however, are rarely needed, even in cultures where hexes are more common, since your enemy would have to be incredibly stupid to waste time and energy throwing curses at someone who has shown the ability to handily remove them.

FIVE

━━━━⊰•◦◉◦•⊱━━━━

Spiritual cleansing, banishing, and exorcism rituals

Spiritual cleansing

In some cases, you may find that there are magical effects that mimic those of a curse, but the curse has not been placed by a magical practitioner. Instead, the hexlike effects are caused by lingering negative energy, which usually has come about from a terrible event having occurred surrounding a person, object, or place. For example, a home in which a murder or rape took place may have lingering energy that causes fear or misfortune. Likewise, an engagement ring from a failed relationship may cause a break-up in subsequent relationships in which the ring is given as a gift, even though nobody specifically cast a spell on the ring. Some people may tend to collect negative energy from emotionally charged experiences, which will be explored further in the next chapter. If not properly psychically shielded, negative energy can hang around, and the person may benefit from performing a personal spiritual cleansing.

Spiritually cleansing a person

Personal spiritual cleansing is not a mysterious ritual that only a skilled practitioner can perform. In fact, everyone automatically and subconsciously performs spiritual cleansing upon themselves all the time, because negative energy is naturally present in our world. However, just like other healthy habits, some people may neglect their spiritual cleanliness in times of stress. Just as you have to take time to prepare nutritious food and make the effort to schedule enough hours for sleep, you need to pay attention to your everyday spiritual hygiene.

AURA CLEANSING

I must include aura cleansing, because this is a service frequently offered at exorbitant prices by professional magical practitioners or psychics, but it is precisely the type of simple upkeep that most everyone tends to do for themselves every day without conscious thought. Recall the section earlier in this book on perceiving auras in order to verify that a curse is present. The idea behind aura cleansing is that effects of negative energy on the aura can be perceived, and that those effects can be eliminated or mitigated through visualization.

First, you'll need to know what an aura that needs a cleansing would look like. In the chapter on discovering a curse, you'll remember that a cursed aura may have dark spots, thinning, or places where the pendulum does not move, particularly around the head. These signs may also be seen in an aura that is simply affected by negative energy. In addition, you might notice dark or thinning spots in other areas of the body, especially those that are injured or a source of illness. Signs of an aura that needs cleansing are much more subtle than a hexed aura, so try perceiving your aura regularly, and if you notice a significant change that seems to be associated with emotional or other life challenges, consider performing a cleansing.

Again, performing an aura cleansing is deceptively simple. Even if you do not "see" auras, such as those of you who prefer feeling with your hands or using a pendulum, visualize your aura as a halo of light around yourself. If you don't see aura colors, you can choose a color that you associate with healing; blue is a common choice. Gradually fill any thinning or dark spots in your mind's eye with the brightly colored light. Many people find that it helps to physically touch the aura with their hands to effectively wipe the dark spots off, collect them, or pick them out, and dispose of them harmlessly back into the earth. A classic technique is to wipe off the dark spots using a raw egg, and then crack the egg into a bowl to examine the contents. If a fresh egg becomes rotted by the aura cleansing, it can be evidence of a curse, but be warned that a clever charlatan performing a trick on you can easily switch the egg for a rotten one behind your back.

Another tool that is sometimes used for aura cleansing is incense. In this case, incense such as white sage is burned and the smoke is wafted over the body with the hands or a feather as if the element of air were washing the person clean.

Using your hands alone is sufficient to cleanse any aura. Imagine the light as dynamic, like a circulating cloud of smoke, in which the movement is uniform throughout the aura. When you can hold the image of a healthy aura in your mind, relax and know it is done. Aura cleansings can be performed in seated meditation, during a spectacular ritual, or in the morning in front of the bathroom mirror while you are brushing your teeth. Practice makes aura cleansing more quick and easy.

ABLUTION

Ablution is the practice of physically washing oneself for the purposes of spiritual purification. Ablution is found across many cultures because of its incredible efficacy and is required before prayer or ritual for many faith traditions. The idea is to make the washing into a visualization and spiritual practice, just like the aura cleansing. Ablution isn't your average everyday bath; it is performed mindfully in order to feel fully clean both outside and in.

If possible, prepare a soaking tub full of water and bath salts. You can make other additions to the water if desired. Milk has been a common bath additive for beautification and spiritual cleansing for centuries. An herb used in several faith traditions for purification is hyssop, but if you don't have any on hand, you can simply use plain water with a little bit of table salt added. When taking a spiritual bath, dunk yourself at least once so your entire body is submerged under the water at once. You can sit and soak in the bath longer if you like, to relax, meditate, and pray. When you feel refreshed, you can end the bath without any further fanfare.

If you don't have a proper soaking tub handy, you can give yourself a sponge bath with a heated bowl of water laced with salt or other additives suggested above. When sponging yourself off, start from your midsection and clean upward as if you're wiping the bad energy out through the top of your head. Then start again at the midsection and wipe downward so that you are washing the negative energy out the bottoms of your feet. In a pinch, sprinkling even your clothed body with water or just washing your hands and face can be acts of ablution if done mindfully or with prayer and meditation.

Spiritually cleansing an object

In the section on hex removal above, where an object is cured of a hex with earth so that it can still be used after the hex removal, the practice shown could also be considered a spiritual cleansing with salt and earth, if the prayer was either omitted or modified to request a spiritual cleansing instead of a hex removal. You can also spiritually cleanse an object in water with an accompanying visualization of the negative energy leaving the object, but be mindful that the salt water does not corrode a metal object or destroy something made of paper. It is okay to rinse salt water off and dry an object after the spiritual cleansing has been performed. If necessary, you can also seal the object in a waterproof plastic bag before washing it in water and salt, since the physical washing is symbolic of the spiritual activity that you are performing with your mind.

Spiritually cleansing a place

Spiritual cleansing of a place may be needed if a negative event such as a crime or an emotional argument happens in the place. However, spiritual cleansing of a place may also be recommended before moving into a new home, or before an important ceremony is to take place, such as a wedding, just in case something negative happened in the place that left residual energy there. Unlike curse removal, spiritual cleansing is something that can be performed preemptively as a precautionary measure. It is also a good idea to look at chapter 6 on hex prevention to learn to cast a circle in the place before spiritual cleansing and to learn to bless the place afterward.

There are two ways in which a place is commonly "washed." One is with incense, and the other is with a floor wash. For incense, I like to use white sage for spiritually cleansing a person or place. Walk counterclockwise around the space three times while wafting the incense with your hand. If it is a building you are cleansing, I suggest covering the general floorplan counterclockwise in addition to walking through every room. You can also choose to walk the exterior of the building and the boundary of the property three times counterclockwise, depending on how thorough you'd like your cleansing to be. Generally, only the interior of a building in which negative energy has taken hold need be spiritually cleansed to rid the area of the effects.

Magical floor washes are used to spiritually cleanse a room or building of ill effects. Traditionally, salt scrubs have been used, although these can be damaging to modern paints and hardwood floors. I recommend using a vinegar-based floor wash for spiritual cleansing due to its natural antiseptic properties as well as the history of vinegar's healing magic. Here's a quick story about it.

During the Black Plague, it was said that four thieves worked out a magical recipe for a potion that protected them so they could rob the dead and dying. The story has entered the realms of mythology in which the recipe and other details vary wildly between storytellers. However, modern concoctions of "four thieves vinegar" usually honor the story with one herb added for each thief. I like to make four thieves vinegar by diluting the vinegar by about half with water and adding lavender, rosemary, sage, and thyme. Keep your four thieves vinegar in a dark bottle to preserve the herbal properties. To use it, you can apply the potion directly to a mop, sponge, or rag to clean floors in a generally counterclockwise pattern of movement. I suggest applying a tiny bit in an unseen location first to make sure that the vinegar doesn't corrode your floors. (I had some stone counter tops in a bathroom that reacted nastily to the vinegar!) If your floors are carpet, feel free to spray the vinegar on the carpet with a spray bottle and, when dry, vacuum.

Banishing rituals

A banishing ritual is a special kind of spiritual cleansing for a place that is performed when the negative energy that is in a place takes the form of an entity. You don't need to diagnose the exact nature of the entity before banishing it, and it is beyond the scope of this book to provide a field guide for every kind of oogity boogity that might make its presence known and unwanted in your personal space. However, I will go through a few cases that are more common in modern Western culture so you can more easily recognize a situation that requires a banishing ritual. Keep in mind that there are a myriad of spiritual wildlife that live all over the world that may not fit these limited descriptions, but all will respond to a banishing.

Ghosts

Ghosts are the remaining spiritual form of a deceased person that hang around a place after death. Not every death may result in a ghost. There are many theories behind what circumstances allow ghosts to form here on earth, and I suspect that many of them may be true since ghosts are actually pretty common, but most of them simply don't make a nuisance of themselves.

It may be that some ghosts choose to remain on earth because of "unfinished business," because of sharing an important message, or because they are looking after a loved one. These are the prevailing theories in popular culture today. Many cultures believe that the timing or manner of death, such as suicide, may cause an incomplete separation of the soul from the body and create a ghost. Other cultures believe that being a ghost is a natural part of nearly every person's life cycle, so that he or she can serve as a helpful ancestor before departing to other realms. Finally, it may be that some ghosts are created maliciously by a magical practitioner who binds the spirit of an enemy to a place or to an object called a fetter in order to punish the enemy or to guard the space or object.

A particularly memorable case of a ghost I was called in to banish was one in which a depressed man had committed suicide in the home in which his family still lived. Unfortunately, they did not have the means to move and still had to occupy the home after his death. However, his widow immediately felt that his presence was still there, and she was extremely emotionally distraught.

I arrived on the scene with my mother, both of us already feeling comfortable with the practice of banishing negative energy from a space. I hadn't yet met the widow, so I wasn't sure whether to expect an actual haunting or simply a woman who was struggling with grief and harboring delusions of a ghost. Stepping into the family home was like entering another universe. Cheerful decorations and tidy surroundings did nothing to mask the energies of that place, which made me shiver and squint despite the heating and lighting being normal. The widow greeted me solemnly and invited me to do whatever I wished. Then she left to stand on the back porch of the house for the duration of my work.

As my mother and I moved through the house praying and working our magic, I caught sight of the man reflected in windows and mirrors, and felt the sensation of pressure and temperature changes brushing oppressively against me. The family dogs, which were contained in the garage, started a furious racket of barking and howling. My mother later told me that she felt frustrated with the ghost burdening his family in such a way and making such a nuisance of himself, and was thinking "shame on you!" internally toward him during the ritual. After the banishing was completed, I moved through the home again to seal out the ghost (as will be instructed later) and I could see that the dogs and widow were visibly more relaxed.

Thankfully, the ghost was successfully banished from the home, and the wife and kids felt an immediate sense of relief. She sent many thanks my way in the days and weeks following the ritual, and was able to move on with her life in that home more comfortably. I can still remember how wildly the man's dogs were barking during the banishing ritual, and how quiet they became after it was done.

How do you know if it is a ghost that is pestering you? Ghosts can take visual form for many people, but the visual form varies widely between individuals, from vapors to skeletons to ordinary human figures. For a more definitive answer, look for the actions of the ghost. Does the entity make noise or appearances just after dark in one room of a house? Does the entity sing a particular song, walk up a certain flight of stairs, or show up in a specific mirror or window? Ghosts tend to repeat or replay patterns from their lives, so if the entity only performs certain activities repeatedly at certain times, like a broken record, you are probably dealing with a ghost.

Elementals

Elementals are naturally occurring but mischievous entities associated with the elements of earth, air, fire, or water. Elementals are unlikely to move into a place uninvited, but they may persist if a home is built on a natural site where elemental presence was strong. Elementals can also easily be enticed, either accidentally or on purpose, into a fetter or a place by a magical practitioner. Some people can see elementals, but again they can take different forms depending on individuals, though they always are associated with one of the four elements.

How do you know whether it is an elemental you have on your hands? First, if the place is a structure recently built on natural surroundings, it may have indigenous elementals. If the place has been used for magical rituals, it could be that an inexperienced magical practitioner failed to dismiss an elemental that he or she invoked. If negativity around the place repeatedly has to do with one of the four elements, such as flooding, mysterious fires, sinkholes, mudslides, or localized high winds, an elemental may be at work. For example, I once knew of a building inhabited by a fire elemental that suffered three unexplained fires in a week. Likewise, I know of a friend who neglected to dismiss a water elemental during a ritual, and suffered broken pipes and basement flooding due to high rainfall in the same day. If your home or office seems like it has more than its share of natural disasters, you may be dealing with an elemental.

Demons

I include demons as a catch-all term for any entity whose effects seem primarily negative in nature. Demonology is a field of study all its own that has its basis not only in the Judeo-Christian faiths, but also in other traditions around the world. I recognize that not all people believe in demons, or in the concept of "evil." However, that does not invalidate the very real experiences that some people have with what they are certain are demons. Even though my own faith tradition does not recognize demons or any source of pure evil, I have encountered people who struggle deeply with violent and dangerous entities they know only as demonic, and I have successfully exorcised the influences of such entities from their lives.

The symptoms of a demonic intrusion into a home or other space has been described to me by clients as being associated with a heightened sense of fear, anger, and other negative emotions in the occupants, as well as violent acts such as scratches appearing on the arm from an invisible enemy, or experiences of feeling a physical attack of a demon before sleep. Please note that demonic occupation of a place is different from demonic possession, which will be addressed in the section on exorcism.

As a side note, medical issues can mimic some of the physical effects of hexes, and the presence of demons in this case. Unexplained appearances of scratches or bruising when a person has no memory of getting injured may be a result of a seizure disorder, for example. Likewise, many historical cases of a demon attack before sleep have been attributed to sleep disorders. The classic case is of a feeling of heaviness on the chest and the inability to move, which may be accompanied by the hearing of voices or seeing dreamlike images in the alpha-wave brain state before sleep. Demons that were thought to cause this sleep paralysis were called incubi or succubi, male or female respectively, and were thought to rape their victims. It turns out that the chest heaviness and sleep paralysis are both common symptoms of sleep apnea, a serious medical disorder. If any physical symptoms occur that you think may be attributed to demons, go to a doctor first to get a checkup. It won't hurt to have a physical evaluation, even if the demons are real. Seizure disorders and sleep apnea can be life- or health-threatening. The brain can be deprived of oxygen, and the afflicted person is commonly deprived of sleep.

How to perform a banishing ritual

A banishing ritual may seem complicated at first, but it is only because it contains elements of cleansing as well as some protective measures to make sure the entity doesn't return. Think of it as similar to the exclusion of a pest animal. First, you'll need to chase the critter out of the area. Then you'll need to seal up any holes and make the place less hospitable so it won't just come right back inside the moment you are finished.

Step 1.) Establish psychic shielding and the protection of a magic circle. This process is useful, particularly if you are afraid of being possessed or harmed by an entity. In situations in which violent effects have been witnessed, please make sure that you read through the hex prevention chapter to make sure you can protect yourself before getting started. It can be helpful to cast a magic circle around the entire space in which you are doing the banishing, but it is certainly not required.

Step 2.) Sweep. Sweeping the area is a special type of cleansing. Unlike using a floor wash to purify negative energy with a spiritual disinfectant, sweeping is used to physically move a negative entity and its associated energies out of the area. Even if the floor is carpeted or the area planted with grass, a broom can be used lightly over the floor or surface of the grass. Before you get started, if you are indoors, open all the doors and windows so you can sweep the energy right out of the building. Walk counterclockwise through the space three times, sweeping the floor. Some also like to sweep the air at mid-level and above the head as if removing invisible cobwebs. Experiment with your sweeping technique to figure out what feels right for you. To make sure the broom itself isn't harboring negative energies, do not use any plain old broom sitting around. You should buy or construct a special broom used exclusively for spiritual purposes.

Step 3.) A banishing prayer can be spoken as you sweep, or directly after, if you have trouble concentrating mindfully on both actions at once.

PERSON LISTENING
*Hail, [God(s)/Goddess(es)/Spirit/
Universe/Higher Self/etc.]*

RAISE PRAISE
*You who is/are [list three
positive attributes], I praise you!*

ASK FOR HELP
*Thank you for banishing [entity]
from [place] and protecting it.*

YOUR DEADLINE
Now.

IMPERATIVES FOR SAFETY
With harm to none, and for the
highest good of all. So may it be.

NOTE OF THANKS
In return, I offer you [gratitude/
love and devotion/other offering].

GRACIOUS ATTENTION
Blessed be. (Pause and be receptive.)

Step 4.) Cleansing. Walk through the area counterclockwise three times, first with incense such as white sage, and second with water with a little bit of salt added to it. If you cast a magic circle before starting the banishing, you may use the same incense and saltwater. These two cleansing materials contain all four elements: water and earth in the salted water, and air and fire in the incense.

Step 5.) Set up a warden. Protection is necessary to keep the negative entity from immediately returning. Banishing is set up through steps 3 and 4, prayer and cleansing. Now is the appropriate time to set up a warden, which will be explained in more detail in the section on hex prevention. If you have performed a banishing inside a building, I suggest putting a bit of garlic on any windows, doors, or mirrors you can, as this protective herb blocks some entities from using these entryways back into the place. When I banished the ghost of the suicidal husband from the home mentioned above, I saw him appear in some decorative mirrors in the home before I applied the garlic. Some believe that unprotected mirrors can act as portals to the spirit world, which is not to say that mirrors are bad in the home. Some choose to mount additional mirrors on the outside of doors or facing doorways in order to reflect out negative energy.

Step 6.) A blessing of the space can now be performed if desired. The banishing has already successfully taken place, and in a sense the cleansing was a type of blessing. However, the space is clean and relatively empty of influential energies. Some believe that filling the space with positive energy can add protection and attract good energy and entities through the magical Law of Attraction. The blessing can be done simply through another prayer, or you can use the blessing instructions from chapter 6.

Exorcism

An exorcism is very similar to a banishing, but it is performed on an object or a person that is being affected with the presence of a negative entity. The only way to tell if an object or person is plagued by an entity, as opposed to simply being negatively charged or cursed, is by someone witnessing a person or creature associated with the effects. In my experience, by the time my services are required, cases of possession or fetters are usually very clear, with frightened people having numerous anecdotes about fighting or fleeing an entity.

How to identify a fetter

A fetter is an object inhabited by a negative entity. A fetter may have been naturally selected as a home by an elemental, the most frequent case being an earth elemental that is enjoying a glittery stone in a piece of jewelry. In the case of some ghosts, a fetter might be clung to by the deceased due to its special meaning during life. Again, jewelry of sentimental value is a common fetter for ghosts, as are musical instruments, furniture pieces, cars, or other objects about which the ghost cared deeply or the ghost associated with a loved one during life. Other fetters might be a cage for any type of elemental, ghost, or other entity placed there by a magical practitioner.

An object may be a fetter if it is associated with negative effects when used, and if a spiritual creature or person is perceived as using the object or appears in reflective surfaces on the object. For example, a piano serving as a fetter for a ghost may sound a note late in the night when nobody is around. A crystal pendant acting as a fetter for an earth elemental may show glimpses of a creature within. Jewelry fetters may disappear from jewelry boxes for days at a time, only to return just as mysteriously.

How to exorcise a fetter

Exorcism of a fetter, like a banishing, contains elements of cleansing as well as optional additional steps such as blessing, if desired. Since a fettered object contains an entity that can be freed immediately, one need not use a lengthy earth cleansing to bleed out negative energy or allow a curse to run its course. The benefit of all exorcisms is that they are instantaneous!

Step 1.) If you are afraid of an entity like a demon leaping out of a fetter and into yourself, by all means, go ahead and perform psychic protection or cast a magic circle as directed in chapter 6, on hex prevention.

Step 2.) Cleansing. Use the cleansing tool that is most practical for the object at hand. You may wish to wave some sage incense over the fetter and sprinkle it with a bit of water with salt added. You may wish to submerge the object in salted water, if corrosion or size of the object isn't an issue. You may wish to give the object a sponge bath with salt water or four thieves vinegar. If the fetter is a large object, a broom sweeping may be the most practical.

Step 3.) Prayer.

PERSON LISTENING
Hail, [God(s)/Goddess(es)/Spirit/
Universe/Higher Self/etc.]

RAISE PRAISE
You who is/are [list three
positive attributes], I praise you!

ASK FOR HELP
Thanks for exorcising [entity] from
its fetter and protecting this [object].

YOUR DEADLINE
Now.

IMPERATIVES FOR SAFETY
With harm to none, and for the
highest good of all. So may it be.

NOTE OF THANKS
In return, I offer you [gratitude/
love and devotion/other offering].

GRACIOUS ATTENTION
Blessed be. (Pause and be receptive.)

Step 4.) This is the protection portion of the exorcism. By now, the entity has been released from the object and it is no longer a fetter. Again, the prayer and cleansing offer protection. However, you may also choose to scratch a protective symbol into the surface of the object or draw the protective symbol in black ink or with a bit of the salt water used earlier. A suggested symbol is a pentacle. This is a five-pointed star surrounded by a circle that is known to have protective effects.

Step 5.) We conclude with the blessing. If you choose to use the object after exorcising it, you may wish to bless it for its new purpose with another prayer, or by looking at the section on talismans in chapter 6 if you wish to use it as a talisman for protective purposes of your own.

How to identify a case of possession

Possession occurs when a spiritual entity enters a person, either of its own accord or because it was invoked there by the person possessed or by another magical practitioner. Not all possession is a bad thing, and many faith traditions include invocation of deities or spirits as part of worship or magical practices. However, when possession happens to a person against his or her will, or when possession persists after a person no longer wishes to be possessed, an exorcism is needed.

Accidental possession is quite rare in modern Western culture. The most likely scenario for possession is a botched ritual where an inexperienced magical practitioner attempted to invoke a deceased person or a demonic presence, or an especially sensitive but inexperienced person takes part in a ritual where spirits were being actively invoked for the purposes of possession without realizing the danger. I have witnessed several cases. One involved a tourist who went to an Afro-Caribbean ritual in which spirits were invoked and became subsequently possessed by a mischievous spirit. I exorcised a person who believed he was possessed by a demon after traveling in another country, as an attack by a magical practitioner. Another case involved a person who attempted to invoke a demon for a black magic spell of his own. Still others had tried to communicate with deceased loved ones through spirit boards or other techniques and inadvertently invited possession.

So how do you know whether you or somebody you know has been possessed? Cases of possession are usually quite frightening and obvious to the person involved and those who surround him or her, insomuch as they won't be mistaken for an ordinary hex or just having a really bad day. Victims of an unwanted possession won't act as they typically do, and they may put themselves in danger or great discomfort by eating unpalatable or inedible things, speaking in a strange voice or language, or even changing appearance or performing physical feats that seem beyond the person's normal capabilities.

The experience of being unwillingly possessed may feel like "missing time" or blackouts followed by regaining consciousness in strange circumstances, wearing unusual garb, possibly having acquired injuries, and having no memory of the unusual acts performed during the period of unawareness. Again, I must repeat the warning that signs of cases of possession, as with cases of an infestation of entities in the home or another place, can be easily confused with symptoms of serious illness. Before attempting exorcism, the potential victim should head immediately to a doctor to rule out seizure disorders, brain tumors, organ failures, serious mental illness, or other physical or psychological maladies that can cause hallucinations and altered perceptions.

How to exorcise a possessed person in theory

I remember the first time I was honored with the duty of performing an exorcism on a person. He came to me seeking me out as a professional psychic who was also openly involved with witchcraft. He told me that he was possessed by a demon. Being not of a Judeo-Christian background, I didn't believe in demons, but I agreed to meet with him at my local library to see if I could talk some sense into him. He had roused my sympathy when describing his long battle with illness. When we did meet, I was surprised that he did not turn out to be some drug-addled lunatic. He appeared to be a respectable professional and a family man. I was rather embarrassed to be giving spiritual advice to somebody who was obviously much more mature and educated than I. As he described his suffering, I realized that he was not just seeking attention or having some kind of mental disturbance.

In my personal practice of witchcraft, I had exorcised objects quite frequently as a matter of course in ritual contexts, so I figured I would take a crack at it, but emphasized to him that I would not charge him money for the service. At a later date, I performed the steps described here. I worried that they would not be impressive enough to him, and that he would think I was mocking him or wasting his time. But during the process, there was a noticeable change in the mood of the room, my ears seemed to pop with air pressure fluctuation, and I was able to actually see a flash of some sort of shadowy form flee the area. The man was immediately thankful. Later, he tracked me down and handed me an envelope that contained a thank-you card and a generous—and quite unexpected—gift of money.

How you can exorcise a person

After a person has been thoroughly checked out by a physician to rule out serious illnesses that can mimic the signs of possession, an exorcism can be performed. In some cases, it can be simple enough to ask for the entity to leave immediately, since an inexperienced person may not have thought of such a basic solution. The steps below are basically the same if performing an exorcism on yourself or on another person, with notes as to any suggested differences. Yes, it is possible to perform an exorcism on oneself. Please make certain that you always have the person's permission to perform an exorcism on another.

Step 1.) We start with shielding. As usual, psychic shielding and possibly a magic circle as instructed in the chapter on hex prevention may be desired if you are exorcising another person and are fearful that the entity within the other person might enter you. Psychic shielding is not required before exorcising yourself, although it may be a good idea afterward.

Step 2.) Banishing. Much like the sweeping that happened during the place banishing ritual, a banishing is performed to open the gates, so to speak, and to usher the entity away from the affected person. As with the exorcism of an object with a pentacle, I recommend drawing banishing pentagrams around the person to start. If you are the affected person, pentagrams can be drawn around you on your own. If you are helping to exorcise another person, have him or her sit or lie as you walk around in a circle. Start by facing east and drawing a pentagram with your pointer finger in front of you, visualizing its formation in blue flame. Start down low and to the left and draw upward to the first point and draw a five-pointed star, ending with a sixth line double-tracing the first line that you drew. That pentagram is now a portal that will draw the entity through it and away from the person, but you will create portals in all four cardinal directions. As you turn in place or walk a circle around the person, visualize a bright blue flame springing up in a circle surrounding you. Turn to the north, west, and south respectively to visualize and trace additional pentagrams.

Step 3.) Cleansing. If you are performing an exorcism for another, you should request that he or she take a cleansing bath before the ritual, and you should as well. However, after banishing, the cleansing should be performed again. I suggest wafting white sage incense over the affected person. Keeping windows open when doing the exorcism indoors will not only aid ventilation for those who dislike pungent incense, but will allow the entity to escape the room quickly.

Step 4.) Prayer. This prayer can be said during the cleansing, if you can do so without distraction, or may be said directly afterward if you need to read notes. As with hex removal, you may say the prayer for yourself, and if comfortable saying for another with his or her higher power(s) in place, please do so in order to help the person feel comfortable and use his or her own spiritual connections to cast out the entity.

PERSON LISTENING
Hail, [God(s)/Goddess(es)/Spirit/
Universe/Higher Self/etc.]

RAISE PRAISE
You who is/are [list three
positive attributes], I praise you!

ASK FOR HELP
Thanks for exorcising [entity]
from and protecting [name].

YOUR DEADLINE
Now.

IMPERATIVES FOR SAFETY
With harm to none, and for the
highest good of all. So may it be.

NOTE OF THANKS
In return, I offer you [gratitude/
love and devotion/other offering].

GRACIOUS ATTENTION
Blessed be. (Pause and be receptive.)

In the case of performing an exorcism for another, I encourage any theatrical embellishments that may put authority
behind the ambiance or the power of your words. You don't
have to go overboard with costuming and lighting, but it pays
off in efficacy if the other person feels confident in the process.
A weakened will, in the case of magic and spiritual entities, is
metaphorically like a weakened immune system in the face
of an infection. Here is another prayer example showing how

you can put a little fire behind your words. Use this technique when performing a hex removal for another person if you feel it will increase their confidence and help that spiritual immune system.

PERSON LISTENING
By the ancient powers of [God(s)] above,
[God(s)] below, [God(s)] within,

RAISE PRAISE
Who creates in the east, dwells in the north,
destroys in the west, south fires set spin,

ASK FOR HELP
Cast out [entity] from [Name]
and guard [him/her] fast,

YOUR DEADLINE
Be it done in this instant, and eternally last!
I exorcise thee, I exorcise thee, I exorcise thee!

IMPERATIVES FOR SAFETY
For the highest good of all, and with
harm to none. So may it be. It is done.

NOTE OF THANKS
I offer gratitude and service returned, and if
that [entity] has not learned, by my will and evil
spurned it shall by itself be burned.

GRACIOUS ATTENTION
Blessed be. (Pause and be receptive.)

Step 5.) We close with the protection and blessing. You may draw a pentacle on the forehead of the affected person with salted water for protection. If desired, now can be the time to give the person a talisman, as discussed further in the chapter on hex prevention. An optional blessing can be performed for the person if he or she has need to heal from illness, or desires greater positive magic in life.

DANCE OUT YOUR DEMONS:
AN EASTERN EXORCISM METHOD

Dance has been a traditional form of invoking entities as well as exorcising them since prehistory. Since, during ecstatic dance, the human soul is thought to be able to leave the body, such a trance state can also be used to expel unwanted spirits or other entities from a person. One traditional form of dance exorcism that may have originated in Africa and spread to the Middle East where it is still practiced today is a Zaar.

The idea behind a Zaar is that a sickened or afflicted person has been possessed by a malevolent entity known in the Middle East as a djinni, the equivalent to a demon for the purposes of this book. The victim is surrounded by drummers and other musicians who play various rhythms until the djinni inside him or her cannot help but dance. As the victim dances a wild possession dance, often characterized by rolling of the head and flipping of hair when performed today, the musicians speed up the tempo of the music. When the djinni is exorcised, the cured person collapses to the floor, exhausted but free and strong of spirit and energy so as to make the immediate return of the djinni impossible.

I have performed Zaar dances not only to exorcise myself of mere negative emotions, but also as a free community service when I empathically take on the burdens of others. I don't recommend a beginner perform the latter, as this has the potential to take on the demons of others. However, if you yourself are possessed, a simplified version of a Zaar can be performed regardless of your dance experience. All you need is a lengthy recorded piece of music that starts out slowly and increases tempo to a frenzied pace, or you can have a friend beat a drum faster and faster until you stop dancing. A suggested Middle Eastern rhythm is called *ayoob* (notated dum/a-tek-tek), which you can think of as beating a drum to the rhythm of the phrase "stretch and faster" over and over again, where the word "stretch" is held as a longer beat.

There are three phases to a Zaar, and the dance can be performed in a group with a leader ringing a bell to indicate the transitions. The first phase of the Zaar is the community phase, where you begin by simultaneously acknowledging your community and dance space while also withdrawing from it into your own body. Begin dancing very slowly, even simply by walking through the room in order to develop a trance in which you are focused on the rhythm. If performed in a group, the community phase can be done in a follow-the-leader line. At the end of the first phase, each person carves out a circle of space to himself or herself in the room.

During the second phase of the Zaar, the music should still be slowly paced enough for you to get comfortable dancing in a small circle. You can use a limp step movement with one foot up on ball and the other flat, or whatever movements you feel called to perform. Move first in a circle, then in place, and focus on moving all parts of your body in a circular way. When the tempo of the music increases, it is time to move into the third phase, during which the exorcism will take place.

During the third phase of the Zaar, focus on allowing your body to make movements from the inner core outward. Movements may take the form of hands flinging from the chest outward, feet kicking, or even larger trunk movements in which you curl up and then spread out. Be careful not to hurt your neck or spine if you get enthusiastic with the outward flinging of energy. Continue with this final phase until the tempo increase or duration is such that you find yourself getting tired, then lie down carefully on the floor to ground the energy and rest until your heart rate and consciousness return to normal. Whatever entity was afflicting you has been paid off in full, and has departed joyfully and harmlessly for other realms. Get up from the floor slowly when done and try to eat a light meal and rest. It is best to perform a Zaar with somebody else in the room to help you if you are overwhelmed by the intense experience.

SIX

HEX PREVENTION

Of course the ideal scenario in life is to not get hexed in the first place. Thankfully, the vast majority of people on earth go through life without having a real, effective, intentional hex ritual performed against them. Earlier in this book, I explained some simple spiritual hygiene techniques that everyone performs at least subconsciously on a regular basis, like aura cleansing. In this chapter I'll go over another regular spiritual upkeep, shielding, that is something we do naturally every day. Shielding can be used for daily protection, even by those who have never been exposed to a hex threat. I'll also go over some more rituals that can be done if you believe that you are a potential hex target, although for most people advanced hex prevention isn't necessary, and may just cause you to become paranoid and devote too much energy to fear. As you go through this chapter, assess what steps are necessary, what steps may be just fun to try, and what steps may be needlessly complex or impractical.

Avoidance

You don't need any fancy charms or spells to keep yourself out of trouble if you can avoid getting hexed at all. Hex avoidance doesn't mean that you have to worry about travelling to foreign countries, studiously avoiding the indigenous people there who practice black magic. However, it does mean keeping your distance from people who hex in your own community and with whom you are more likely to come into frequent contact. If you know a person who is into malicious magic *and* starting drama with others, it's best not to invite him or her to your magic rituals, potlucks, or other social gatherings. Avoiding situations in which you make yourself a target through threatening or provocative speech and behaviors is another strategy that will keep you safe and draw more mature people to enjoy your company.

Who gets cursed and why?

In my experience, aside from the cases of curse scams in which a random victim is selected from the clientele of a crooked psychic or other magical practitioner, most hex victims are not cursed by people they do not know. The type of people who get cursed are often nice people who may not hold their tongue when they see somebody doing something they do not like. Don't get me wrong, I can identify with being a blunt person, but picking fights with a known black magic practitioner can lead to magical retaliation. In fact, the common thread I've seen in most genuinely hexed victims is that they are no strangers to magic themselves, but usually have been either benefitting from magic performed on their behalf by others, or are magical practitioners who work in a group.

Witch wars and conflict resolution

In the chapter on what to do to a person who hexes, I listed some ways that you can react, set boundaries, and perhaps even resolve a conflict with an individual who has hexed you. I'd like to go a little more in depth with what to do if you are a magical practitioner, or if you work in a group of such people, like a coven. A coven is a group of witches who work together to worship, practice magic, or both. In a group context, certain personality conflicts will inevitably emerge, and they can create an environment conducive to starting a never-ending "witch war" of back-and-forth hexes and animosity.

It's high time I told my own hex story, which began in a coven context. I was working with a group of people who cast beneficial and helpful spells together. Though I knew that one of the older and more experienced members used to practice black magic, he was now working with our group, which rejected such practices. We gladly allowed members to sit out if they felt even slightly uncomfortable or negative about a spell.

It was not even in the setting of magic ritual that my conflict with him began, but in social gatherings we all attended as friends. The more experienced members of the group had strong, authoritative personalities and often had respectful disagreements about any topic under the sun. I myself was several decades younger than the other members, and I can't deny my long-standing tendency to undermine the authority of others. On several occasions, I criticized the behavior of my friend one-on-one and in front of others during our social outings, which turned him into an enemy. At last, he could take my disrespect no longer and chose to leave the group. I was surprised, since my youth and arrogance made me largely oblivious to the fact that I had offended him.

Shortly after his departure, I noticed him appearing in my nightmares. These nightmares plagued me constantly and affected my sleep patterns. At first I didn't mention them to anyone, but finally I confessed my tribulations to some of the more wise members of the coven, who recognized that the dream intrusion he was using was something he had bragged about doing to others in his shady past. They removed the hex and applied some of the hex prevention strategies that follow. In hindsight, I realize that when I first began having problems with this fellow, who was more experienced than I and well established in the group, I should have asked another member to mediate our dispute and resolve it openly. Instead, I created a petty and negative undercurrent that climaxed in my enemy leaving us and then retaliating against me.

If you find yourself practicing magic in a group setting, know that there will be strong personalities involved. One strong personality every group should have is at least one respectable leader who has wisdom and perspective. If your group doesn't seem to have someone in this role, leave it immediately. Be aware of one or more troublemakers in the group, commonly known as trolls. Trolls are known for "patrolling." They look for opportunities to assert their strong opinions and even put down others in order to try to raise their status in the group. And yes, in the story above, I played the part of the troll.

THREE SIMPLE STEPS FOR
DEALING WITH A TROLL IN A GROUP

Step 1.) It is okay to pull the troll aside for a one-on-one discussion about your differences, if you feel safe doing so. However, if you already fear that he or she may hex you, or resort to physical or emotional violence, you can skip this step. Use your "I" language to express how you feel and to request help from the troll. Maybe you want to set boundaries, like "please don't call me on the telephone between meetings" or "please use my first name when referring to me" if name-calling is a problem. Don't repeat these one-on-one interactions if your first attempt to resolve the issue doesn't end well.

Step 2.) Request that a leader of the group sit with the two of you while you brainstorm a resolution. Try again to meet with your enemy along with one or more leaders of the group. If you consult with an experienced leader, you may find that the group has specific procedures for dealing with interpersonal conflicts that can save you a lot of headache. You may also find that your enemy's demeanor is far more amicable when leadership is present during a meeting. Allow the leaders to drive the conversation as much as possible, and if you are asked to speak, continue focusing on your own feelings and suggestions about how the leadership and your enemy can help you in the future.

Step 3.) If all else fails, leave the group. In some cases, magical groups are a democracy in which procedures dictate that members can vote out a troll, which may give you an opportunity to oust your enemy. In other groups, you have to "vote with your feet" by leaving, if you don't like the way that things are going. I have had to leave groups myself, and each time was painful to have to walk away from the people I loved and with whom I had always had pleasant interactions. However, leaving can be the most mature option before you cause such dissention that you and your enemy break up the group entirely. Take heart that if a troll is the reason for your leaving, most trolls are unstable people who will leave of their own accord soon after you have made your departure, at which point you may be able to return, having saved face and avoided a major blow-up.

Protection magic

Protection magic is a strong part of every magical tradition, even those that don't include hexes, since our world is naturally full of challenges and dangers. In this section, I will explain a number of different protective techniques that can be used together or separately, depending on your need and comfort with the different tools at your disposal. Think of all of these as gadgets on your superhero belt that can be deployed according to the situation.

Daily Devotional Prayers

Again, I turn to prayers as a first line of defense when protecting myself. You can set an alarm each day to remove yourself to a private place to pray, if you like, or you can say your daily devotions silently to yourself in the shower each morning. Prayers can be a big production or a simple routine. Do whatever feels most natural. Following is another sample prayer in the format given earlier.

PERSON LISTENING
Hail, *[God(s)/Goddess(es)/Spirit/*
Universe/Higher Self/etc.]

RAISE PRAISE
You who is/are my loving,
protective guardian(s), I praise you!

ASK FOR HELP
Thank you for defending my body,
mind, and spirit from hexes,

YOUR DEADLINE
Now and forever.

IMPERATIVES FOR SAFETY
With harm to none, and for the
highest good of all. So may it be.

NOTE OF THANKS
In return, I offer you [gratitude/
love and devotion/other offering].

GRACIOUS ATTENTION
Blessed be.

Pause for three deep breaths to wait for a
message or a sign, which is especially important
during protective prayer since a warning
may come to you, which you can use that day.

Psychic shielding

Psychic shielding is a way to create a barrier between yourself and negative energy on the astral plane. Shielding is something that everyone does, to some extent, quite naturally. If you are able to perceive auras, you will be able to notice someone else's aura fluctuate depending on whether their guard is up or down. Part of what you see in a person's aura may be the person's psychic shield. However, just as keeping an aura clean and dynamic can sometimes take mindful work, it can be hard to keep your psychic shield up at appropriate times, especially if you have a very stressful job. For example, high school teachers are the targets of negative energy hurled by growing adolescents all day long. If a high school teacher is unaware of the practice of psychic shielding and also doesn't naturally keep his or her shield up during teaching hours, a career change may be in the not too distant future.

So how do you practice psychic shielding on purpose? If you are able to see auras, I suggest that you start by observing your own aura. Take a look at the chapter on detecting a hex for how you might begin perceiving auras. Get in front of a mirror and try to see your own aura. Close your eyes and imagine yourself in a safe, intimate setting, surrounded only by people you love and trust. Open your eyes and notice how your aura has changed. Has your aura expanded and become more fuzzy, or has it almost disappeared entirely? Now close your eyes and imagine yourself in a more stressful situation in which your defenses have to be up, such as a job interview or a past situation when you were dealing directly with a bully. Open your eyes and observe how your aura has changed. Have the edges of your aura hardened or taken on a specific shape or color? Has your aura expanded or contracted when you started to defend yourself? If you were able to perceive your aura, you can now visualize the way your aura looked or make yourself feel those feelings again in order to put up a strong shield against your enemy's onslaughts. Practice in the mirror until you can put up a psychic shield instantly.

Even if you don't physically see auras, you can still use visualization to generate a psychic shield. In fact, even though I do see auras, I began using visualization to generate a shield one day after my normal shielding suddenly seemed to stop working. I could still see my aura, but I felt vulnerable, and the people in my life who were psychic vampires suddenly started getting into my personal space and on my nerves. On the advice of an older and wiser friend, I started using a visualization that looked entirely different from my aura, and it worked perfectly. Your shield can take any form that you can imagine, as long as being within it offers you a sense of strength and defense against whatever onslaughts the universe might throw at you. Here are a few common (and uncommon) shields I have seen used.

- A bubble creating a thin film you can see through but that nobody can penetrate without your permission.

- A rainbow shield. As energy passes through each layer, negativity bounces away and only the positive aspects of the energy are allowed through.

- A ring of white or purple light creating a column around you from the ground up.

- A circle of flames surrounding you wherever you go.

- A suit of armor, coffin, or sarcophagus cocooning you from all danger.

- Your body grows and takes the form of a power animal like a bear or a snake to ward off enemies.

- You are surrounded by a pack of hounds, a pair of wolves, or other animals that guard you.

As you can see, the possibilities are endless and limited only by your imagination. The things you create in your mind's eye will exist on the astral plane, and thus interact with energies that are sent to you on that level. Even if you feel a bit silly with a visualization, try it in a public setting and note how other people react. Do they pretend that you aren't even there? Do they act intimidated by you? Do they keep a respectful distance, or do they seem to draw uncomfortably close? The way that you present yourself in your mind's eye affects the way that others perceive you and interact with you. Practice shielding on a daily basis so that you feel comfortable projecting a powerful shield the instant you sense a threat.

Casting a magic circle

Now that we've gone over some simple techniques that don't require any theatricality, I'd like to go into a ritual technique that can take more effort: casting a magic circle. A magic circle is a space that is defined here on the physical plane as well as in the astral. A magic circle is most often cast to temporarily contain energies that are being generated for a spell in order to enhance the effects of the spell by releasing the energies all at once. Containment of energy is why casting a magic circle was advised as an optional component to some of the rituals and spells already mentioned in this book. However, I write about casting the magic circle here as a form of protective magic, as the magic circle has also been traditionally used to keep negative energies and entities out of a space. For example, if you are plagued by bad dreams sent to you by an enemy or are as a result of some malicious entity, you can cast a magic circle around yourself and your bed before you sleep and dissolve the circle upon waking. This is an extremely effective measure against allowing those influences into your dreams.

Casting a magic circle is like setting up your own little protective bubble between you and the worlds of the physical and the spiritual. As a result, sort of like when you go camping, you need to bring things with you that you need in order to exist. Symbolically, casting a magic circle creates your own little universe, so you'll need to bring with you some symbols to represent everything in our universe. Luckily, magical practitioners have broken down all the ingredients for the universe into four useful symbols, the elements of earth, air, fire, and water. All you need in order to cast a magic circle are visualizations or physical representations of the four elements. I recommend the common ingredients of salt for earth, incense for air, a candle for fire, and a bowl of water. Of course, you don't want to keep candles and incense lit when you're sleeping, so you can use other representations for air, such as a perfume, a feather, or even by blowing bubbles. Fire can be replaced with an appropriate lamp, preferably red to invoke the image of fire in your mind.

Define a space for your magic circle. You can do so with your imagination alone, or by drawing a line with chalk, salt, flour, or a length of rope. Your circle can be small enough to contain just you in a small dorm-room bed, or large enough to include an entire house and property if you are performing a blessing ritual on the area. As in the banishing ritual, use a broom to sweep your ritual space three times counterclockwise, as the counterclockwise direction is associated with banishing negative energy. You may wish to sweep the floor first, then a few feet off the floor, and finally over your head as you walk.

After sweeping, walk the circle clockwise three times, visualizing setting up a boundary along the real or imagined line that you have defined. Hold out your dominant hand and use your pointer finger as you draw the line. Some people choose to use a ritual knife to point during this phase of casting a circle, which can help keep malevolent entities at bay. If you choose to use a ritual knife, select one that is double-edged with a black handle for protection magic and use it only for ritual and for no other purpose. People's visualizations vary, but you may wish to think of what sort of border says protection and strength to you, like a castle wall or a sphere of barbed wire, before calling it up in your mind's eye.

Next, you are going to purify each of your elemental representations, to rid them of any negative energy, lest you take it with you into your circle. Begin in the north, which is associated with strong, protective earth power. Pointing at the salt with your pointer finger or with the ritual knife, say, "From this earth I banish all negativity and malevolent magic." Hold the salt container up to the north and say: "Welcome, guardians of the north, powers of earth." Visualize the strength of earthquakes and the hardest rocks and metals of the world using their energy to protect you.

Repeat the same sequence for each element as you walk clockwise around the circle. Next comes east. Over the incense or other representation of air, you can say, "From this air I banish all negativity and malevolent magic." Present it to the east, saying, "Welcome, guardians of the east, powers of air" as you visualize the energy of a windstorm that could sweep any enemy off his or her feet away from you. Walk around the circle three times clockwise with your incense or representation of air to sweep the positive energy into your circle.

For south, as you exorcise your representation of fire, say: "From this fire I banish all negativity and malevolent magic." As you show it to the south, saying, "Welcome, guardians of the south, powers of fire," you can visualize the searing heat of fire keeping all of your enemies at bay like a campfire in the night to scare away predators.

Finally, in the west, say, "From this water I banish all negativity and malevolent magic." Before presenting it to the west, you can add three pinches of salt from the north. The mixing of the cleansed salt and water makes a special holy water that you can use for protection by sprinkling it on yourself or anything or anyone else that you wish to defend and banish of negativity. Hold the salted water up to the west and say: "Welcome, guardians of the west, powers of water."

Visualize a cleansing tidal wave of water washing away all malice from anyone who approaches you. Walk around your circle three times clockwise with your salted water, sprinkling a little bit as you go with your fingers, in order to cleanse the space and invite in the positive energies of the elements.

At this point in your circle casting, you have already thoroughly cleansed and banished the area of negativity and invited in the protective presence of the four elements. Before going to sleep if you've cast this circle around your bed to ward off bad dreams, or before beginning to work magic, it is customary to call on any deities or higher power in which you believe. Use a simple prayer to invoke the source of power of your choice.

PERSON LISTENING
I invoke thee, [God(s)/Goddess(es)/
Spirit/Universe/Higher Self/etc.]

RAISE PRAISE
You who is/are my loving,
protective guardian(s), I praise you!

ASK FOR HELP
Thank you for defending my body,
mind, and spirit from hexes,

YOUR DEADLINE
Now and forever.

IMPERATIVES FOR SAFETY
With harm to none, and for the
highest good of all. So may it be.

NOTE OF THANKS
In return, I offer you [gratitude/
love and devotion/other offering].

GRACIOUS ATTENTION
Blessed be. (Pause reverently before
proceeding with your rite.)

Now is the proper time to craft any spells or charms, or do whatever work needs to be done within your magic circle. It is best not to leave a magic circle that is cast for the purposes of protection. If you absolutely must leave to go to the bathroom or take care of other immediate needs, quickly cut a small hole in the circle with the pointer finger of your dominant hand, and upon returning close the hole using your hand in a similar way. While cutting out of the circle does not damage a circle that is used to concentrate energy for spells, it can weaken a circle that is cast for purely protective purposes. Therefore, ideally you should take down the circle entirely and set it back up again later if you want to use it as a means of defense. For that reason, I have kept the circle takedown procedure as simple as possible, so that it can be done in a hurry.

When you are finished with your magic circle, never leave it standing, since entering and leaving the circle space will gradually weaken it. It could also encourage unintended effects from entities such as elementals that are attracted to your elemental invocations. To take down the circle, begin by thanking your higher power, although of course you don't have to send her, him, or them away from you. All other influences from the four elements should be allowed to leave your circle space with a respectful dismissal as you hold your visualization of each of them. Walk to each quarter, starting in the north again and moving counterclockwise to banish energy, holding each element's representation in turn. Say something like the following:

Thank you guardians of earth, return to your realms
of the north to remain ready to defend me.
Thank you guardians of water, return to your realms
of the west to remain ready to defend me.
Thank you guardians of fire, return to your realms
of the south to remain ready to defend me.
Thank you guardians of air, return to your realms
of the east to remain ready to defend me.

Make a final walk around the perimeter of your circle with the salted water and the incense or representation of air, counterclockwise still, to give a final blessing to and from the elements. Now, open your circle with the pointer finger of your dominant hand, as if you were slicing it or cutting it down. You might visualize the circle collapsing or crumbling into nothing, leaving the space as if the circle had never been cast at all, with the possible exception of a nice smelling incense or perfume on the air. Your magic circle is open, but can be recalled at any time. Even if you are missing the tools needed to create a magic circle, you can use your imagination and create the protective effects of a circle without the fanfare when truly needed.

Amulets and talismans

Amulets and talismans are both magical objects that are traditionally carried or worn by a person, usually for protection. For the purposes of this book, I'm going to use the term *amulet* to describe a natural object that is already imbued with protective properties, and *talisman* to describe a charm that is crafted and then charged with the protective energies that are required for it to be able to work.

Some common protective amulets include a stone made of tiger's eye, which traditionally wards off the evil eye associated with hexes, and any stone that naturally has an X on it. For example, a piece of granite with two veins of quartz running through it that cross each other. Another amulet that is good luck as well as protective is any stone that naturally has a hole in it. A "holey stone" can be used not to only protect from danger, but also to warn a person of danger when he or she looks through the hole and takes the first thing seen through the hole as an omen.

If you find a holey stone, try wearing it as an amulet, threading a string through the hole. If you feel a sense of unease, go to some outdoor place and look through the hole in the stone. What do you sense when you watch what you see through the hole? Some people use the movements of birds as a sign that caution should be taken or not. For example, a bird flying from right to left in your field of vision through the hole is a positive sign, while one flying the other way is a sign to be very careful—unless you see an owl, in which case the directions are reversed. Look through your holey stone in many circumstances in order to start learning what signs are good for you, and which show that your day may be filled with treacherous obstacles or dangerous challenges. You may wish to start a journal in order to become proficient with the signs your amulet shows you.

A talisman can be made and then charged within a magic circle simply by visualizing your own personal safety very strongly, perhaps imagining your enemies being kept at bay by your charm. But first, you'll need to decide what sort of talisman to create and then you have to make it. A talisman can be a collection of objects you associate with safety placed in a small black bag. For example, if you have several of the amulets described above, they can be put together in a bag to create one talisman. You can also make a talisman by inscribing letters or symbols on anything, even paper, to add to your bag or to make into a pendant to wear. Again, the best color to use for protection magic is black, so using black ink or black paper can be helpful.

Crosses or the letter X are protective symbols, as are circles. An eye is also a symbol to protect against, of course, the evil eye. In the Middle East, eyes are made of blue glass to be used as talismans. The pentacle, a five-pointed star circumscribed by a circle is also a defensive symbol, representing the four elements as well as your spirit being enclosed by protection. If you have words of power or names of ancestors or other things that give you a feeling of safety, you can make a sigil as described in the chapter on hex removal. There are several other talismans you may find useful that use lettering a little different from the sigils presented in that chapter.

The Sator Square is a special lettered talisman that has been used as a magic charm for thousands of years. It consists of a Latin palindrome, *sator arepo tenet opera rotas*. It can be read horizontally or vertically, and reads the same with all letters in the sentence reversed. Roughly translated, it means "the sower of the seeds spins the wheel"; that is, we all reap what we sow. The magic of the phrase is intended to turn any enemy's negative magic back upon the caster. The Sator Square is written like this and then charged to become a magic talisman:

SATOR
AREPO
TENET
OPERA
ROTAS

Another lettered talisman that has been used since ancient Roman times may make you feel a little bit silly because it uses the word *abracadabra*. Abracadabra is not a made-up word for modern stage magic; it has been used for thousands of years and may be an Anglicized misrepresentation of an Aramaic or Hebrew phrase, *avra kadavrai*, meaning "I have created through my speech." Creating an abracadabra talisman is especially useful for protection against illnesses or injury of any kind if you believe your enemy is targeting your physical health. Write the talisman in a triangular form (as in the following graphic, from the bottom up), increasing one letter each time to represent creation symbolically.

A-B-R-A-C-A-D-A-B-R-A
A-B-R-A-C-A-D-A-B-R
A-B-R-A-C-A-D-A-B
A-B-R-A-C-A-D-A
A-B-R-A-C-A-D
A-B-R-A-C-A
A-B-R-A-C
A-B-R-A
A-B-R
A-B
A

Another simple talisman—one that does not involve lettering—is a tassel. In the Middle East, tassels and mirrors have traditionally been used to distract and hypnotize malicious entities. Any tassel will do, though I suggest making your own with black yarn in a magic circle for maximum efficacy. Simply wrap the yarn over a note card or your fingers many times and then tie a string to fasten all the loops together.

Opposite the string you've tied, cut the loops with scissors so that you now have many short strings bound by a single secure string that will act as your hanging apparatus. Flute the tassel strings downward, and loop a final string an inch or so below the fastener so that the tassel strings won't slip out. You can hang your tassel from your clothing, a bag you carry with you, or even your car's rearview mirror for protection.

If you live in an area that has rowan trees, you can also make rowan berry charms as talismans once a year. Pick the rowan berries just before the fall equinox, but not afterward, for the best of good luck. Thread a needle with black thread and string rowan berries on it as if they were a necklace. I personally like to string 108 rowan berries per necklace, as the number is sacred for performing Hindu chants. In this way the charm can double as a set of prayer beads if I want to select a mantra that I find gives me a feeling of safety.

You can wear your rowan berries, but I find that the necklaces are too delicate for daily wear, so I like to hang mine up in my home and car, out of reach of pets and children. Over the course of the year, the rowan berries will dry out and turn black as they absorb any negative energies. When you make new rowan berry charms in the fall, you can burn the old ones to harmlessly release the negativity they've absorbed.

Wards and wardens

A ward is a spell that is cast, usually upon a place, in order to protect it from enemies of any kind so that they cannot find or enter the place to harm any therein. A ward can be as simple as a house blessing, which is included below. A friend of mine, when blessing her home, visualized it as a beacon that allowed anyone who was meant to visit it to find it easily, while allowing any enemies to become hopelessly lost and unable to locate it. To cast a simple ward, walk around the building or space three times clockwise, if possible, while chanting:

I ward this place
From roof to floor
(or "from earth to sky" if outdoors)
From all sides and doors
(or "from where all borders lie")
Within and without
As the wide world turns about
I ward this place.

A warden is an object imbued with protective powers used in a ward spell. A ward that uses a warden is especially effective, because the object works like a pair of magical eyes for you, watching out for danger and working to thwart it. Do note that wardens require more work than a simple ward; it is recommended you renew your ward twice a year if you have a warden by "feeding" the warden. Traditionally this is done at the first of May, or Beltane, and the end of October, or Samhain. Feeding the warden can be done simply by saying a prayer of thanks or leaving an offering of food and drink if it is a stone or statue kept outdoors.

To create a warden to protect a home or property, select a stone or a statue you wish to use as the warden. Cast a magic circle in order to concentrate the energies with which you want to charge your warden. Come up with a name for your warden, which can be anything you wish. Inscribe the name on your warden in black ink, and visualize your property under its powerful protection. You may even wish to personify your warden as a mythological creature or some other powerful being in your visualization. Finally, say the ward chant, using your warden's name as follows:

[Name] ward this place
From roof to floor
(or "from earth to sky" if outdoors)
From all sides and doors
(or "from where all borders lie")
Within and without
As the wide world turns about
[Name] ward this place.

Open your circle and place the warden as soon as possible thereafter. It is best placed near an entrance, like a driveway or doorway, or in a place where it can "see" much of the property. Feed it twice a year while saying the ward chant once again to renew the ward. Do not remove the warden from the property, even if you choose to move to a new place. You can leave the warden, or you can release it in the same way you might exorcise any other object. You will need to establish a new warden on your new property.

Dream catcher

A dream catcher is a special kind of warden with which you may already be familiar through various Native American legends and modern art crafting. A dream catcher is a warden placed in a bedroom that directs good dreams to a person and ensnares nightmares so they don't enter the dreamer's head. A dream catcher does not require feeding or offerings, although I still think it is a good idea to thank wardens a couple times a year. It has no need for any chants unless you want to perform them. I do recommend casting a magic circle. It will help concentrate your desire for the dream catcher to do its work.

To make a dream catcher, you'll need a circular frame, which can be made with a flexible stick (willow is traditional) bound into a circle, some string, a bead, and any feathers or embellishments you'd like to add to hang from the bottom to let those happy dreams glide on down into your head as you sleep.

Cast a circle and as you create your dream catcher visualize yourself getting restful and pleasant sleep. Start by wrapping the string around the edge of the circle frame, creating relaxed loops of string as you work your way around the circle shape of the frame. When you get back to the first loop, pass the string through it and pull it. Then go on to the next loop, repeating this step around the circle. As you progress, you are catching the innermost loops in the net and bringing them closer to the center of the design. It takes some practice to make dream catchers, so don't worry if your string net is sort of loose and messy looking. Even a messy net will catch those bulky bad dreams. When you get to the middle of your dream catcher, leave a small hole. Tie the string to a loop and tie the bead, suspended in the middle, to act as bait for all of the dreams. Afterward, you can add your embellishments if you wish. Close your circle and immediately hang your dream catcher above the head of your bed. When replacing a dream catcher, you should exorcise it like any other object, and you can burn it.

Witch's bottle

Another simple warden object that comes from ancient origins is a folk magic witch's bottle. A witch's bottle can also be used as a hex removal tool when hair and nail clippings from a victim are added. A witch's bottle is any jar or bottle, preferably dark colored, filled with all sorts of sharp, nasty objects. You might add razor blades, nails, pins, needles, broken glass, and any other sharps to be discarded. The next step is one that many people find distasteful: all members of the household that wish the witch's bottle's protection should urinate in it a little bit. If adult women wait until the time of their menstrual bleeding, urine from that time of the month is best. The idea is that evil is drawn to the bottle, caught by the sharp objects, and then drowned in the urine. If you simply can't stand the thought, wine or seawater can be substituted as a last resort.

Bury the witch's bottle at the farthest corner of the property of the household being protected. Be very sneaky and discreet about the burial, because an enemy need only dig up and smash the witch's bottle to render it ineffective, so make sure that you cover and disguise the burial place well. Do not dig up and remove the witch's bottle when you move. Instead, create a new witch's bottle in your new home.

Bottle tree

Another way to protect a place is to construct a bottle tree. Similar to a dream catcher, the idea is that hanging beautiful bottles that catch the light from a tree in the yard will distract and capture malicious entities. Simply collect interesting and colorful bottles and hang them from strings on a suitable tree in your front yard for a beautiful decoration with protective properties. Note that if you live in a region that experiences freezing weather, you'll have to either use plastic bottles or take your bottles inside for the winter. Otherwise, you'll end up with a lawn sprinkled with shards of glass.

Blessing a place, object, or person

A blessing is a way to protect something, someplace, or some-one by "wrapping" them in positive energies. For example, blessing a space is a wonderful ritual to do after a banishing in order to fill the void that the banishing created with positive energy. When a space is filled with good things, there's no room for the bad. Likewise, the astral space inside a person or object can be filled with blessings so there's simply no room for evil to take hold.

Blessing a place

Generally, a blessing is all that a given space needs in order to make it safe and suitable for habitation, or in order to prepare the space for a sacred event, like a wedding. However, if negativity is known to reside there, a banishing and cleansing should be done beforehand. And, if the space may be a future target for negativity, a ward should be cast and a warden should be placed. I personally like to perform a cleansing if the home has been lived in by somebody before me.

The process of circle casting is also a place blessing, since it calls in the positive energies of the elements and also your chosen higher power. For that reason, I recommend casting a circle over as much of the home as possible. Make sure that over the course of the cleansing and circle casting, you've sprinkled the holy water and walked the incense through every room in the home. I like to use frankincense for blessing purposes. If you've missed any places, go over the entire home again with the holy water and incense.

When blessing a new home or office, I like to place a penny in each corner to draw in wealth and abundance as well, although this step should be omitted if you have small children or pets that might swallow loose change.

Try not to bring an old broom to a new house. Leave it in your old home and purchase a brand new broom for your new home in order to leave behind old energies. Discard any brooms left by previous occupants.

Blessing an object

Now that you have learned to cast a magic circle, blessing becomes very simple since you make holy water over the course of casting a magic circle. The combination of the calling of blessings from the elements and your higher power, as well as the touch of air and fire from incense and the touch of earth and water from the holy water, will bless any object. To bless an object, exorcise and cleanse it first if necessary, and then cast a magic circle and make sure to put the object through the smoke of the incense and to sprinkle it gently with the holy water, wiping it if afterwards it could corrode or be otherwise damaged.

Blessing a person

Like an object blessing, a person can also be lightly censed with frankincense and then sprinkled gently with holy water after any needed exorcism or cleansing. The only difference is the need to explain the process to the person first, and to make sure that he or she will not be sensitive to the scents and rituals you will be using. Allowing a person to take a bit of your holy water in a bottle and sprinkle it around his or her own home is a nice touch for a blessing ritual. You can also use the holy water to make your own blessing oil for daily anointing. Add a few drops of the holy water to grapeseed oil with more of your salt from the north. Some frankincense resin should also be added and allowed to soak in the oil from at least one full moon to the next. A person can dab the oil on his, her, or another's forehead in the shape of a pentacle for protection.

Diverting a curse harmlessly

Another way to prevent hexes is to divert the course of a hex, so that it is absorbed by the infinitely forgiving earth or, perhaps better still some might think, so that it is reflected back upon your enemy in its original form. However, diverting a curse can be a lot more challenging than hex removal or avoidance, since you will have to know when you are being actively targeted by somebody in the process of casting a hex, and you will have to be very proficient with diversion techniques such as grounding and reflecting energy.

The power of grounding cannot be underestimated. I encourage you to reread the section on grounding if you are new to it. Practice grounding at least once a day until you can ground at a moment's notice, even in a distracting and emotionally provocative environment. If you are truly good at grounding and employ it the moment you first feel the effects of a curse, you can actually act as a conduit for the negative energy to pass quickly through you and into the earth, where it can be harmlessly dispersed. Even if you think you have grounded a hex effectively, please perform a divination to check that you are truly free from it. If you aren't, you will need to perform a hex removal to rid yourself of any residual energy. A diversion can be bungled if you started grounding too late or ended grounding too soon.

Reflecting negativity is another skill you can employ using a form of shielding. I have already mentioned using a mirror visualization to bounce a hex right back at its caster. With a strongly visualized mirror shield, you can easily deflect a less experienced magician's hex attempts. In the process, you might also make him or her regret trying to hex you when that energy comes flying right back in the same form it was sent. A friend of mine likes to use the visualization and analogy of returning a letter to its sender unopened instead of a mirror, which works in the same way to deflect the hex without coming into contact with it.

Mirrors have been used on clothing and in homes and other buildings for protection magic because of their ability to reflect negative energy. However, since they also have the potential to act as portals for spirits and other entities, I recommend putting a bit of garlic on any mirrors you mount in your home for protection, to add to the protective power. Try hanging a mirror on the outside of your front door or just inside your door facing the doorway. Doing this will reflect back on anyone standing on your stoop the same energies they want to bring into your home. Wearing a mirror on a necklace or buying a scarf or article of clothing with mirrored embellishments can also act as effective talismans. However, remember that the mirrors as talismans are tools for your mind, so using an effective mirror shield visualization can be just as effective if you can do so strongly and in an instant.

Become a healing activist

As you near the conclusion of this book, I hope that you feel empowered to deal with hexes in many ways. You may find that hexes are usually a figment of the imagination, your own or another's. You have learned that hexes are easily removed, and can be diverted, warded away, or avoided entirely. As soon as you feel confident enough to deal with potential curses for yourself and for others, you may notice that there are many people in your life who fear curses, either real or supposed. Instead of laughing them off, you are now equipped to address common fears and concerns head-on, and you can become a source of healing for somebody who is truly suffering. I'd like to wrap up this book with a few suggestions about how you can make the planet a better place, spreading blessings and reversing curses wherever you go.

Ridding the world of curse scams

It is my greatest hope that the information contained in this book will help to destroy some of the ongoing curse scams. The idea that I could help clients avoid these pitfalls inspired me. Though it would be terrific for all curse scams to be outlawed, such legislation would be difficult to enact without impinging on freedom of religion and of speech. It would be even more problematic to enforce, since banning hex extortion can take away the right to hex, which can, in effect, cast doubts on the legal status of psychics. Instead of quashing the rights of all, I believe the best defense against the spread of fear and misinformation is the spread of knowledge and courage within all of us to stand up for what is right.

Fight back if anyone attempts to victimize you with a hex scam. Take a look at some of the legal and practical steps you can take in the chapter on what you can do to somebody who hexes or runs a curse scam. Even if you were not fooled by the charlatan, somebody who is less savvy than you might be taken for all he or she is worth. You must fight criminal behavior when you see it, for the good of the most vulnerable members of your community.

Don't allow anyone you know to be taken by a potential hex scam. If you even suspect that somebody you know is being scammed, step in, be nosy, ask questions. You might be tempted to let an elderly loved one spend money however he or she wishes, if it makes the person happy and doesn't seem to cause any harm, but remember that there may be others who are less financially able to deal with such a scam who are suffering unduly because such con artists are allowed to thrive. Look in the section of this book on how to talk to a loved one about hexes in order to find suggestions for intervention.

Finally, should any of you reading this book decide to set up shop as a professional psychic or fortune-teller, be sure to report other supposed colleagues who take advantage of clients through hex scams. Encourage victims to come forward to the proper authorities as necessary. Be open about your revulsion for hex scams, and have an open policy about removing hexes for free. This will ruin the economic viability of extortion schemes. If enough clients and professionals make the cost too high and the payoff too low, we can effectively rid the industry of hex scams.

Dispelling myths and fears

Hexes and curses are the stuff of nightmares and legend, and are shrouded in mystery, which makes them even more potent in the minds of those of us steeped in popular culture. Very few people in our modern society know true information about black magic. Rumors and fear can spread in a community like wildfire. In the famous play *The Crucible*, Arthur Miller gives us a glimpse of the insanity of the Salem witch hunt, as panicked teenagers cook up wild fantasies and end up accusing a perfectly innocent person of practicing malicious magic. Such illogical and pointless destruction of community and the lives of innocent people is not just relegated to the past. As you've learned from the chapter on bad luck, there are plenty of logical fallacies built into the human mind that can cause one to leap to conclusions about black magic.

Even though it may feel awkward, volunteer what you know about hexes when people voice their fears, laugh uneasily about their worries, or speak in hushed voices about their concerns. It may be tempting to laugh it off, especially if you know that the hexes that they fear are not real. However, since the suffering is real, and since real complications can happen as a result, it is best to share your knowledge. Speak up bravely about black magic, as you would to prevent any other type of bullying. When you meet someone who believes they've been hexed, let them know that there are specific steps one can take to protect oneself from further hex effects.

Blessing the hexing and the hexed

You may want to take the next step toward being a healing activist. Volunteer your time and energy to curing the hexed. You will benefit not only from the positive energy that you send out to the world, but also from the great practice in the art of magical defense you'll receive. Even if you openly advertise yourself as removing hexes for free, you won't be inundated by people looking to waste your time or to take advantage. I have been vocal about hex removal for over a decade, and have come to find that those who believe that they have been hexed have generally not been at all, and those who have been hexed can be freed from their suffering with very little effort on my part, either to educate them or to eliminate the hex myself. I highly encourage people with the proper training to freely offer hex removal, spreading the word and thereby making the world a better place.

There is a simple but far less intuitive (and perhaps more emotionally difficult) solution to the problem of hexes in the world. This is to send out blessings and positive energy to your enemies, and to all those who hex. Killing your enemy with kindness is one excellent response to somebody who hexes you. The blessing energy bestowed can cancel out and block negativity in the same way that an excellently planted garden can inch out the weeds. Be cautious with your prayers, even to wish somebody well, because to infringe upon somebody's free will is to create a powerful binding that you don't want applied to strangers on a daily basis. If you wish to bless an enemy, you'd do well to ask his or her permission, to show your good faith. If you wish to send out energy to any potential hex caster who needs it, ask that it be freely given only to those who wish to receive it. I'll leave you with an example prayer that can be added to your daily devotions.

PERSON LISTENING
Hail, *[God(s)/Goddess(es)/Spirit/*
Universe/Higher Self/etc.]

RAISE PRAISE
You who is/are loving, forgiving
and healing, I praise you!

ASK FOR HELP
Thank you for rescuing the cursed and soothing
those who hex, if they wish to be helped.

YOUR DEADLINE
This day and every day.

IMPERATIVES FOR SAFETY
With positive energy sent to all those who need it,
to be used as they will with harm to none,
and for the highest good of all. So may it be.

NOTE OF THANKS
In return, I offer you my service as a
healing activist and hex remover.

GRACIOUS ATTENTION
Blessed be.

Pause for three deep breaths and listen for a sign from
your higher power about somebody in your life who
may need your help to alleviate suffering.

What should I do to a person who hexes?

Immediately after finding out that you or somebody you love has been hexed, the next obvious response besides fear and a desperate search for hex removal is probably anger and a desire for retribution. Don't feel guilty if you experience a sense of hatred and dark thoughts of harming somebody who hexed you. Even a minor hex can feel like an extreme violation of your body, mind, and spirit. You may even wish to consider receiving counseling to work through your residual emotions so they won't plague your life. It won't do you any good to ignore your need for validation and justice. What can ease your mind is to learn more about what happened to you and what can happen in the future, so you'll feel more in control of the situation. In this chapter, we'll explore more about the sort of people who do cast black magic spells, and what you can do about it besides removing hexes.

What sort of person casts black magic?

In popular culture and media, the sort of person who practices black magic is portrayed as a villain, sometimes even played by a character with exaggerated and ugly features. Reality isn't as simple as the bad-guy-versus-good-guy trope, however. Practitioners of black magic have families and people who love them, and may have day jobs and live relatively normal lives. I'd like to describe a few of the black magic practitioners I've known for those of you who may have never met such a person other than on a movie or television screen.

The first sort of black magic practitioner that comes to my mind is the type for whom magic is a tool, and black magic is part of a lifestyle and culture. As mentioned earlier in this book when I first described hexes and how they are performed, I noted that there are many countries and cultures in the world in which hexes are commonplace. Instead of one mysterious villain at work making black magic, magic may be used like any other tool in life by men, women, and children.

For the vast majority of people steeped in our familiar Western culture, if somebody threatens a family, the victims call the police or defend themselves with fists or weapons, or whatever blunt instruments are within reach. For somebody proficient with magical spell-casting, a hex is just another blunt instrument that might always be within reach. Even if you feel like you are the victim of a hex, a person who hexed you may feel like they have been victimized, or that they are protecting their families or livelihood from potential harm by you. Such a misunderstanding can easily cause anger and escalate. And just as in cultures where gang violence is rampant, a cycle of vengeance can emerge and last for generations.

Another sort of black magic practitioner that comes to mind is one that is far less effective. This is someone who turns to black magic because of its exotic nature, rather than because it is a familiar tool. Such a person might be an experimenting teenager, a depressed and downtrodden person who feels a lack of control in other areas of life, or a spiteful ex or family member who turns to black magic because the alternative of physical violence is much easier to track and to legally prosecute.

Although such people might be intimidating, especially if part of the power trip is for them to dress and act like the villains you see in movies, they are actually far less dangerous to you than a more skilled practitioner for whom magic has always been a way of life. In fact, you can rest assured that such a person is likely to cause damage to themselves not only through living a life of spiteful action, but also due to inexperience working with the dangerous tool that is black magic.

Evidence that a person practices black magic

Before I jump into a series of clues that somebody may be a practitioner of black magic, remember that just because somebody can cast spells doesn't mean that he or she feels it's worth the time and energy to cast any sort of spell on you. Just as it would not improve your life to be afraid of anyone who practices martial arts or goes target shooting with a rifle, you aren't going to benefit from freaking out every time you meet somebody who knows how to make magic. Also, I have to include the obvious disclaimer that people do break stereotypes. For example, even though some Christians and Wiccans may feel it is against the rules of their religions to hex, they may break the rules.

Racial profiling doesn't work so well for the police, and it won't work too well for you, either. Even though there are cultures and countries in which hexing runs rampant as a practice, it is not easy to determine someone's cultural origin. And even in cultures steeped in black magic mythos, there are plenty of people who would never touch the stuff. However, this shouldn't stop you from using logic to deduce that a girl who's lived in modern American middle-class suburbia for the entirety of her teenaged life lacks credence if she claims to be well versed in black magic as a Haitian witch doctor or Vodou Mambo priestess.

The biggest piece of evidence you can have for whether a person is a practitioner is how he or she acts when claiming that you have been hexed. It is likely that a black magic practitioner will actually tell you that you have been hexed, because it does no good for him or her not to do so. At the very least, his or her feelings of defensiveness or retribution would, they hope, be validated with a fearful reaction. A skilled magical practitioner is more likely to deliver the message calmly to you, especially if he or she shows up at your home or workplace with the sole purpose of delivering the message, since it is more likely that the hex ritual has already taken place during a full or waning moon, or that final arrangements are being made such as a magical sigil, figure, or other artifact being left near you. If that person or any person exhibiting unusual behavior attempts to touch you or your food or drink, or leave an object behind, be on your guard.

A competent magical practitioner will likely have his or her life put together. If you think about it, if such a person has the power to hex enemies, then he or she must also be able to bless and heal. In many magical systems, certain rules are followed to protect the practitioner from losing his or her power. You may notice that the person never eats around enemies, or avoids grounding by only eating light and unsalted meals. Magical laws are such that words have power, so some magical practitioners strive never to lie, and may as a result seem oddly selfless, even to their detriment, or blunt in social settings when it comes to telling the truth. Most of all, look for a person with a very controlled mind who seems to be able to contain or unleash emotions at will and on a moment's notice.

If you are able to see or sense auras, you have another valuable energetic tool to be able to determine whether somebody is not only a competent magical practitioner, but one who is on his or her guard against you for whatever reason, which would be evidence that he or she feels engaged in some sort of energetic battle with you. Take a look at his or her aura and try to sense energies toward you. A competent magical practitioner will have a clearly defined and vibrant or intense aura.

If he or she is feeling defensive when around you, the aura will draw more closely inward around the body than most people you see, especially around the midsection and head, so that you may perceive a slight pear shape. I don't want to limit this warning to precise colors, because many people perceive aura colors differently or don't see them at all; also, the colors may vary due to the type of misfortune the person wishes to deflect or project. However, the shape surrounding the body is important. Energy centers related to survival are located low, around the rear end, while those that project and sense emotions are in the midsection, which your enemy may wish to contract or withdraw in self-protection.

Evidence that a person is not an effective magical practitioner

Again, using common sense is the key to detecting when somebody is lying about having trained in the magical arts. If an enemy refers to magic in the context of the countless ways it is portrayed in popular culture, if it's the kind depicted in movies or on television, then he or she is just trying to scare you. Refer to the previous section, where you learned how to spot a genuine practitioner, and look for the opposite kind of behavior or appearance. An ineffective magical practitioner will have obvious failings in life such as financial difficulties, an inability to form healthy relationships, and deep unhappiness. Remember, if a person has the power to hex, he or she should be able to solve most of their own personal problems with such a magical tool.

Most phony hexes are hurled by exes, friends, or family members—idle threats made in the heat of passion. It is therefore unlikely you've been hexed by an effective magical practitioner if a person impulsively yells that you'll be hexed. From time to time, everyone says things they don't truly mean, but consider that having such an uncontrolled emotional outburst proves that the person cannot master mind and spirit well, and probably lacks the control to cast even a simple spell. Think of such threats as similar to empty legal threats made by people in situations where both of you know they have neither the funds nor the evidence to make a case against you, and relax.

If you have the ability to see auras, you can sense the energy of an ineffective magical practitioner as fuzzy, large, diffuse, and not clearly defined. The shape of the aura may be round, radiating from the midsection if somebody is lashing out at you in anger. The body energy centers around the abdomen flare up when somebody attempts to get a rise out of you and sense your reaction. The swollen and poorly defined aura is a result of their own uncontrolled emotions allowing their energies to spread away from the body as anger is projected outward. If you are a sensitive person, you may wish to shield yourself against anyone with such an aura, as described earlier in this chapter. Generally, as long as a person remains in such an excited state, they will not have the focus and willpower to be able to cast a real and effective hex on you.

Extortion schemes

I have already written at length about psychic scams and false hexes claimed by people who will charge a hefty fee for a bogus hex removal. It is also important to know that there are some out there who will cast *real* hexes and then demand money for hex removal, although such circumstances are much more rare, since they require a huge investment in energy and an assumption of risk on the part of the perpetrator. Therefore, I'd like to tell you about the sort of person who uses a hex scam to make money, so you can be empowered and armed with more knowledge. Usually such petty criminals operate in the dark, and are consequently steeped in mystery, which only enhances fear.

One of my clients who had been taken for a ride by a psychic scammer found the scammer just down the street from her house. The scammer ran a small herb shop, and her business card advertised that she removed hexes and returned lovers. When my client went to see her, the scammer suggested that my client had been experiencing health problems, which happened to be true; my client had experienced some issues with her digestive system and was thinking about going to see a specialist about it. The scammer said there was no need, and that a curse had been placed on her by a jealous ex-lover. My client thought that sounded reasonable as well, since she had recently gone through a messy break-up. The scammer seemed like a nice lady who was seriously concerned for my client's well-being. She also had small children running around in her shop and was a neighbor, so my client trusted her more than a stranger. The scammer said that she normally charged a thousand dollars for hex removal, but for my client, she would reduce the price to a hundred and perform a smaller hex removal. Unfortunately, the hex removal didn't seem to work, and my client had to return to her. The scammer kept requesting larger and larger amounts of money, which my client kept paying since she had already invested so much. Suddenly, one day when she returned to the scammer, the whole shop had been closed and the scammer had disappeared from the neighborhood with everyone's money.

Remember that scammers and criminals are regular people too, with families and a need to earn a livelihood. It may be easier for people with a need for food, shelter, and support for their loved ones to be able to rationalize making a living off of the misery of others. For example, some may come from a long line of people who run the same scam. To them, fooling people into believing in a curse is no more "evil" than a stage magician dazzling his audience with tricks or a horror movie director frightening children who watch the movie late at night.

Less common but more dangerous is the sort of person who casts real hexes for money, either from a client wishing to harm an enemy, or in order to extort money from a random victim. Again, these are not supervillains, but people skilled with using a tool that may have been a way of life in their family and in their community for generations. If your enemy becomes a client, he or she is often also an acquaintance at the very least. They bring a sob story and a bundle of money. The magical practitioner, although a professional, is often sympathetic to the cause, since he or she only hears your enemy's side of the story. If, however, the professional is running an extortion racket by cursing random victims and then demanding payment for a removal, this practitioner has entered the realm of criminal behavior. There is no excusing an act of violence of any kind, but there's no sense overdramatizing it, either. Like any other violent crime, hex extortion is rare, the risk of its occurrence can be minimized, and its perpetrators can be brought to justice.

How can I find out who hexed me?

If you've been victimized by a genuine hex, it is a given that you will want to know who was behind the attack. In fact, you may have to reign in your immediate anger and curiosity to focus on the more immediate task of hex removal. Focus on the task at hand. Please don't jump to this section and work on finding the culprit before you have safely removed the curse and verified that it is no longer harming your life or the lives of others. It's not bad to want to know who hexed you; it's common sense that you would want to identify the dangerous people in your life to feel more secure and to know whether somebody you trust has been betraying you. A targeted defense against a specific enemy is also much easier to handle emotionally than always being on your guard against a potential curse.

I recommend divination to find out who has hexed you. Revisit the earlier chapter in this book that described some of the various divination tools that help to confirm whether you have been hexed. Each of these tools can also be used to find out who hexed you. To use the aura sensing method, make sure you've read the previous section on how to tell if somebody is an effective or ineffective black magic practitioner. Though it is beyond the scope of this book, crystal ball reading is an extremely effective way to see your enemy's detailed features or at least symbols associated with him or her, so if all else fails I highly recommend that you read my book *Crystal Ball Reading for Beginners* if you are unfamiliar with other forms of scrying or seeing pictures using a divination tool.

In general, most people I know who have been hexed already have a pretty good idea of who might be their attackers, and need only confirmation. If not, the pool of potential enemies can at least be narrowed down so that a divination tool can simply indicate the most likely culprit. If you are already proficient with a divination tool such as the tarot, a card can be laid down for each potential enemy to seek confirmation. Even the inexperienced can use a tarot deck and a book of interpretations to find out which card most likely indicates the culprit. If you don't already use tarot cards and don't want to learn an entire complicated system, fear not. There are other ways to find out who hexed you.

If you only need confirmation, a pendulum can be an excellent tool to use. Remember to calibrate a pendulum each time you use it by first asking "show me what yes looks like" and "show me what no looks like." Wait and watch the pendulum for the different movements or lack of movement associated with those answers. Then you can ask the pendulum, "Did _____ knowingly place a hex on me?" Wait for your answer, and take the immediate first response that comes from the pendulum. Don't wait until the answer changes, even though it may be tempting when you really want a positive answer but receive a quick negative response.

If you have two or more potential enemies, you can hold the pendulum over representations of them, such as photographs. For example, if you have three ex-girlfriends who might be the type to cast an effective hex (and by the way, if you do, you have very interesting tastes in women), lay out a photograph of each one on a table. Say to the pendulum, "Show me who hexed me." Then slowly move the pendulum over each photograph in turn, waiting for a result. Be careful not to swing the pendulum with your hand while you move between photographs. You want to have a very steady hand and a very slow transition between photographs. Wait for a response over one of the photographs. If none of them indicates a positive result, then you have confirmed that none of the people pictured are at fault.

Palmistry would be a lot more effective if you were able to stare closely at the palms of your enemies, but since it is unlikely that a skilled magical practitioner would let you do that, all you can do is look at your own palm. Earlier we explored palmistry in the section on determining whether you have been hexed. I explained that although a star in the palm doesn't always mean a hex, it certainly *should* be present if you *have* been hexed. The location of the star on your palm can help you find out who did it, or at least in what realm of your life you see the enemy who has cursed you. First, find the star on your palm, then check to see whether it is near the following reference points.

Neighbor: If the star on your palm is on top of, touching, or very near an oddly colored patch on your life line, which is the line on your palm that curves around the base of your thumb to your wrist, a neighbor could be the enemy. Likewise, if the star is on or touching a line that branches from that life line up toward your middle finger, somebody in very close proximity to your home may be the one to watch.

Coworker: If the star is near or touching a line that runs the length of your palm from your middle finger right down the center, a person with whom you work could be hexing you because of personal conflict or a desire to get ahead, unless you suspect a paternal figure.

Boss: Like a coworker, if the star is on top of a line that runs to your middle finger, especially in the upper half of your palm, your boss or an authority figure at work may be the enemy at large.

Friend or ex-friend: If you have a friend who is trying to work against you, the star will appear next to or touching the outside of the life line, the side farthest away from your thumb, as it curves downward.

Lover or ex-lover: If you are freaked out about an angry ex, he or she may be represented in two ways on your palm. If the star is touching a cross that is found low on your palm underneath your ring finger, that ex may be at fault. Another place to find an ex is a mark along the heart line, which is the top-most of the main horizontal lines on your palm, and it is there where you will also find the star.

Wife or ex-wife: Like a lover, a wife or ex-wife can be a cross under the ring finger, though usually more near the top of the palm, so the star should be touching that cross. A wife or ex-wife can also be a horizontal line coming from the percussive edge of the hand directly underneath the pinkie finger, with that star touching it of course.

Husband or ex-husband: Same as the signs for a wife or ex-wife above, or he can also be a line coming up from the lower percussive edge of your hand to either your middle finger or ring finger. Look for a star touching either the cross or one of those lines, if present.

Grandmother: If you have an angry grandma who is willing to cast a hex on her own grandchild, the star will be found on the fleshy mound at the lower percussive edge of your palm.

Grandfather: A star that indicates your grandpa is at fault can be found in one of two places, either low on the palm on a line that goes straight up to your middle finger, or on a branch from that aforementioned line that is right underneath the middle finger.

Cousin: In some families, love/hate relationships can form between cousins. If the star is found just above the big fleshy mount at the lower percussive edge of your palm, you can suspect a cousin at work.

Sister: If your sister is cursing you, the star may be found at the very base of your palm on the percussive edge of your hand.

Brother: If it is your brother who is to blame, the star will be at the very base of your palm on the thumb half of your hand.

Mother, mother-in-law, or stepmother: If the star is found on a pink or red line on that big fleshy mount on the lower and percussive side of your palm, it could be a wicked stepmother at work.

Father, father-in-law, or stepfather: A paternal figure can be represented by a line or branch from a line that goes straight up and down your palm under your ring finger. If you have a star touching that line, you might have to put a paternal figure or male authority figure at your place of work on your suspect list.

Children: Directly underneath your pinkie finger, you may have horizontal lines coming from the percussive edge of your palm. Your children are perpendicular lines that jut up and down from those horizontal lines. If you have an angry teenager getting into black magic and hexing you as a result, a star will touch one of those lines.

If no amount of divination makes it clear who hexed you, don't fret. You needn't actually know who it is. You can always protect yourself from hexes in general. Reread the earlier parts of this chapter to set your mind at ease. If you still have trouble finding closure, please consult a therapist or counselor so you can work on letting go of the fear and blame surrounding the anonymous violation that happened to you.

Legal, physical, or spiritual actions you can take

First of all, I should state that if you are looking for legal advice, you won't find it here. I don't claim to be a lawyer. If you feel you have been victimized, either by a fraudulent hex scam or by an actual person attempting to harm you with black magic, the first thing to do is to consult with law enforcement in your area. In both these cases, immediately report every incident of threat to the police. This will create a paper trail of evidence upon which to build a case. From the start it will make it easier for the proper authorities to follow the situation.

The first recourse I would like to address is what should be done when a phony hex is claimed by a psychic in order to extract money from a client with an unnecessary hex removal service that costs an arm and a leg.

ACTIONS FOR PSYCHIC FRAUD VICTIMS

When clients come to me with a horror story of a bad experience with another psychic, they may feel as if they have no recourse for poor service. On the contrary, there are many actions that can be taken, and some are listed here in order from most reasonable and advisable to more drastic and potentially less appropriate for a given situation. Even if you are ashamed of having been tricked or want to put the experience behind you, I encourage you to follow through and protect clients who are more vulnerable, not to mention to improve the reputation of my proud industry as a whole.

- Sleep on it. If your reading was bad news but didn't directly claim a curse or ask for hex removal money, don't jump to conclusions about underlying motives. It can be easy to shoot the messenger. When you're unsatisfied, you might feel hurt and angry, and it is hard to be appropriately assertive when your emotions are running high. You may shoot yourself in the foot when an otherwise peaceful resolution could be reached. Things may feel different in the morning. If you need to vent, write a letter, but don't send it yet.

- Try to resolve the issue directly with the psychic. Calmly explain what your expectations were, why the reading did not meet those expectations, and ask what the psychic intends to do to make things right. Many professionals offer full refunds (unadvertised, so as not to attract unscrupulous clients who have no intention of paying). On the other hand, there may have been an honest misunderstanding and a follow-up may be all you need to be completely satisfied.

- Lodge a complaint with the company if your psychic is a contract worker. If your psychic works for a larger company, website, or hotline, go above the psychic's head if you can't resolve your dispute directly and contact the company's customer support center to request a refund. Many companies have specific policies against hex removal scams.

- Dispute the charge with your credit card company. If you can't get your money back using either of the above methods within thirty days and you used a credit processing service or credit card to pay, your money can be returned directly to your account. You can contact your bank to see what options there are to stop payment on a check or debit card transaction.

- File a complaint with the Better Business Bureau and request their free conflict mediation help. They may be able to get results as an impartial third party. If your psychic turns out to be a fraud, his or her reputation can be ruined in this way and further action can be taken or advised.

- If you feel you've been scammed, contact the police. Fraud is a crime, and if think you have been robbed, file a police report. Remember to contact the authorities in all areas in which the crime took place, so if the fraud works out of another city, you must contact your local police department and the police department in the other city.

- Contact your state's attorney general if you believe a business has scammed you. Fraudulent business practices should always be reported to the attorney general. Again, if the fraudster works out of a different state, contact the attorney generals in your state as well as the state from which the fraudster works.

- If you were scammed via mail, contact the postmaster general. If by advertising, contact the Federal Trade Commission (FTC). Mail fraud is a federal crime. If you report it, the FBI may become involved if necessary. The FTC regulates advertising, so if your purchase included plagiarism, false reviews, or other false advertising, lodge a complaint.

- If you are advised that you have a civil case on your hands and you could not recoup your losses by the actions above, you'll need to consult an attorney to figure out your options of legal recourse. Your community will almost certainly have pro bono lawyers available for your use if you cannot afford one, so find those local resources!

- Warn others. I only include the option of warning others since that is the first vindictive act to which many clients turn after they have been wronged. If all the above avenues have been exhausted, it can sure feel better to try to keep others from falling into the same misfortune. If you received the reading from a site that has a rating system, leave a negative rating with as rational and objective a feedback as you can muster. If you think you've been a victim of a larger, more complex scam, consider contacting local news sources in both the area in which you reside and work and the area in which the psychic works. Post your experience online if you must, but realize that as

with other avenues, if any of your public statements
are found to be speculation or even simply don't have
sufficient evidence to be proven entirely true, you
may have legal action taken against *you*, so resist
the urge to embellish, and stick to only the facts
you can prove.

Things you can do to somebody that you are certain has cursed you

- Move on and live life triumphantly as if nothing ever
  happened. Although it would be nice to see immediate
  justice whenever you are victimized or abused by a
  hex, sometimes the best and most vexing thing you
  can do to your enemy is to show how little the hex
  has affected your life. They say that the best revenge
  is living well, and it's true. Imagine your adversary's
  frustration if, after spending money on a professional
  hex caster or after concerted effort that affected life
  negatively for himself or herself, you simply remove
  the hex the next day and keep walking around smiling,
  as if it never happened. Take heart that the laws of
  magic dictate that justice in the form of similar hex
  effects may afflict the one who hexed you without you
  even having to do a thing. In fact, standing back will
  reduce your interference and keep you out of harm's
  way when the big backlash hits your enemy's life.

- Try to work out a resolution with your enemy. If somebody cursed you that you simply can't ignore forever, such as a mother-in-law, it may be that you can work out your differences and put the violence to rest. You'll need a lot of maturity to try this option, since your focus will need to be on letting go and moving forward to the future of your relationship with this person, instead of retribution or blame. If you are going to confront your enemy, please do not do so alone, as the magical violence may become physical violence. Ideally, you will be able to hire a third-party mediator, such as a counselor or clergy person, to chat with both of you together. Try to avoid mutual friends or relatives who might get caught in the middle and have violence directed at them. Don't ask a friend of yours who is a stranger to your enemy, which might make your enemy feel like you are ganging up on him or her. Together, brainstorm a solution to your dispute, and try to acknowledge your enemy's contributions by paraphrasing and thanking him or her, even if the suggestions are outrageous. With calm discussion, hopefully you can reach a compromise immediately. If not, set a date to meet again and some boundaries to try to keep your distance until then.

- Kill the person with kindness. In addition to taking the steps listed about moving on cheerfully with your own life, find out how you can help out and improve the life of the person who harmed you. This is especially useful if the person who hexed you is a loved one like a child or parent. Figure out what is missing from his or her life and try to offer your assistance. Help can only be truly given if accepted, so don't force your help if it is refused. Simply tell him or her that you are ready to help whenever he or she is willing, and continue to live life happily to show your enemy that you mean no harm.

- Call the police. If your enemy is in a different city or county, call the police in his or her jurisdiction as well. There may be laws in your area that make it a crime to harass and terrify other people, even if members of your local police don't believe in hexes. Even if there is nothing the police can do, filing a police report helps to show that there is a pattern of malicious behavior toward you, which will assist you if your enemy begins to resort to physical violence or vandalism as well.

- Call a lawyer. There may be some simple procedures and paperwork that can put distance and boundaries between you and your enemy. If it is not illegal now for him or her to hex you, breaking the agreements within legal documents may also be breaking the law.

- Shield yourself with a mirror visualization. Using a visualized shield that looks like a mirror in your mind's eye can spiritually defend you immediately. You may remember a childhood rhyme that has floated around: "I am rubber, you are glue: whatever you say bounces off of me, and sticks to you." The idea behind the mirror visualization is the same. By thinking of the mirror in your mind, you create a reflecting effect on the astral plane, which sends back the negative energy to its source. Thinking of the childhood rhyme as you visualize can help you allow that energy to bounce off of you without harm.

- Use ultimatums and communicate clear boundaries to your enemy. First, set up hex prevention and familiarize yourself fully with the mirror visualization above. Then, communicate clearly and assertively with your enemy that you wish the harassment to stop and that you have protected yourself and rendered all hexes useless anyway. You can't control your enemy's behavior, but you can lay out consequences for further harassment, such as calling the police or potentially having his or her negative energy backfire.

- Cut all communications and spiritually cut the cord. More than just moving on with your life, this suggestion entails both the practical and spiritual solution of not only cutting all communication and contact with your enemy, but also erasing him or her from your mind as much as possible by distracting yourself and removing reminders. Working with the magical Law of Knowledge, this forces both of you to have less magical power over each other. The ancient Egyptians would erase the name of an enemy, chipping away the hieroglyphs from their stone monuments, because being forgotten was one of the greatest actions one could take against another. A full cord-cutting ritual is included in the following pages.

- Consider binding. A binding ritual is a special magical spell in which an enemy is prevented from doing further harm. Unfortunately, the downside of a binding ritual is that it magically ties the two of you together. I would advise against a binding if the person is somebody you want out of your life, so only use it on a loved one such as a relative and only as a last resort. A full binding ritual is included below.

- Want to get petty and get even? I don't recommend lashing out and harming your enemy back, not only because of the negative repercussions that can happen to you directly due to how magical laws work, but also because the laws of society will come into play if you turn to violence or emotional harm in any way. While petty retribution may seem tempting (especially when you're angry), I encourage you to take your time if you're dead-set on countering a hex with black

magic, violence, or vandalism of your own. Be sure
you are comfortable with a potential backfire on your
own loved ones or the logical consequences of your
behavior before you proceed, and *please* try all other
avenues first.

WHAT NOT TO DO

Don't drag other innocent people into your squabble. Especially if your hexing enemy is a family member or friend, don't
bring a mutual loved one into the middle of it, and never use
children as pawns when dealing with an angry ex. Not only
will you escalate matters with your enemy, who might perceive you as ganging up on him or her and become even more
defensive, you might also cause harm to the innocent person
caught in the middle. If you need reinforcements, call in professionals if at all possible such as counselors, police, thera-
pists, or members of the clergy.

Don't resort to physical violence, vandalism, or any other
criminal behavior. In fact, such temptations may be symptoms of the hex talking, since calling you out into a life of
crime may be just what your enemy wants you to do. After
all, it is much easier to prosecute you for a simple crime with
abundant evidence than it is to try to use legal means to stop
a person who has hexed someone else. Control your anger;
take the high road.

Don't use social or emotional means of harming your
enemy. To get around the legality of harming the person directly, you might be tempted to call his or her employer and

spill the beans about the black magic or to hold a mutual friend or a child emotionally hostage, forcing loved ones to choose sides. Stop and think clearly through your rage. While nobody may have witnessed your enemy casting a spell on you, if you spread yourself thin trying to cause trouble in his or her family and social circle, you're creating many witnesses to your own bad behavior. Lending credibility to your enemy and alienating yourself from others is only going to harm your recovery from the effects of a hex on your life.

Don't counter a hex with a hex. You knew that advice was coming from how I downplayed a counter-curse as an option in my list on the previous pages, but I have good reasons. First of all, remember that people who are ineffective at magic can have unintended consequences happen because of their magical actions. It is very unlikely that the first hex you ever cast will work, especially if you are not already proficient with magical practices. Your spell could backfire and harm you directly, or even worse, it may harm you and the people you love. Uncontrolled energy has a way of radiating from its source and causing terrible consequences if the intent is malicious…even if you have a specific target firmly in mind.

There are those who believe that the energy you send out into the universe returns to you, sometimes in multiples, such as thrice. If you are working with a magical system that includes beliefs about karma or the Threefold Law of Return, you may be subjecting yourself to those energy patterns and reap negative repercussions, even if you are a very skilled spell-caster. Even if you think that the damages to your own life are worth the feeling of revenge, please consider that there are people who care about you, and seeing your life come apart at the seams will certainly cause them anguish.

Another good reason to avoid a counter-curse is because you could start a magical "witch war," so to speak, which can last generations and spiral out of control. Just take a look at any family feud to see how a relatively tiny wrong can snowball into a violent war that drags in other people who weren't even involved in the original slight. You can't undo the past with your enemy, but you can make sure that you don't begin a cycle of negativity that will continue into the future.

Finally, you may find that there are more mundane downsides to casting hexes. Depending on the laws in your area, you could be arrested and charged. There are still many areas of the world in which malicious witchcraft is treated very seriously by the authorities. Even with lesser charges of a harassing nature, you might end up with hefty fines, incarceration, and difficulty with employment or child custody due to such a history. Once you've made yourself the center of negative magical activity, the social implications can also leave you without friends or alienated from your family. Magic is a powerful tool, to be sure, and just like many other tools, it can be used as a weapon. Even though it may be sneakier and sometimes even more effective to use magic than to use a gun on an enemy, using magic naturally has more far-reaching effects than a single strike with any other weapon, due to energy's eternal effects and the fact that our universe is interconnected through magical energy.

I'd like to share my own personal mistake in dealing with an enemy and a perceived curse that happened to a family member. Now, I should disclose that the family member came to me when I was in my late teens. I was young, stupid, and taking a break from my fortune-telling business to attend college. A family member who knew I practiced magic and trusted my witchcraft more than her own came to me with tales of woe about a curse at work. She explained that somebody at her work was making her life miserable and was doing everything wrong. Even though my family member was the "curser's" manager, she didn't want to fire him because he had a young family; she would feel guilty about taking away his livelihood. I pointed out the obvious: disliking a coworker is hardly a curse, and it's a problem that many people have to deal with.

As she calmed down, my family member agreed that she probably was not cursed, but asked me to perform a spell to help solve her problem all the same. Feeling overly proud that an older family member had such confidence in my magical skills, I agreed. On the full moon, I burned a black candle carved with his name and sent my energy out into the universe, chanting that he should leave his job, quietly hoping he would find a better job elsewhere.

Soon afterward, unfortunately, the young man died in a car accident. My family member sent me gifts of thanks that only made me feel more guilty that perhaps my spell had something to do with it. In hindsight, there were many things wrong with the spell I cast. First of all, I should not have dragged a potentially innocent third party into my magic. For all I knew, my family member was exaggerating her account of the whole situation—maybe *she* was actually the person at fault between the two of them, or maybe it was a matter of mutual miscommunication. Even if the coworker was to blame, I should have only offered to perform magic on my loved one so she could gain more control over her feelings. Finally, even if I did decide to cast a spell on him, I should have been more explicit that he should have better job opportunities presented to him.

Alternatives to cursing and witch wars

I'd like to go into a few of the more common spiritual tools in depth. Here are some rituals that can be performed after an enemy has already begun hexing and has been clearly identified as the source of the black magic.

BINDING

Popularized in movies and television as a magic spell, a binding is done on a specific enemy to prevent him or her from doing harm. Binding rituals, usually done with sympathetic magic upon a doll or picture of the enemy, have been performed since ancient times; bound figures and other artifacts have been found in many cultures. Binding used to be done as a curse in and of itself, since rendering your enemy harmless to defend himself or herself was one way to ruin lives.

Since it uses sympathetic magic and the Law of Association, a binding is an especially energetically taxing ritual to perform. What I mean by this is that as you bind, you are bound. When performing an effective binding ritual, you are using your own energy to tie up your enemy, and so your energy will be tied to that of your enemy forever. For this reason, a binding is a particularly bad idea in the case of an ex-lover, coworker, boss, acquaintance, or random enemy off the street. The only times when a binding may be appropriate are in the case of a loved one to whom you are already tied for life, such as a child.

Since a binding is such a serious "curse" and intended to be permanent, I advise discussing the binding with its intended target first. You may be able to state an ultimatum about binding as leverage in an intervention-style confrontation with your enemy and hopefully come to a different resolution to your problems. Try not to use the binding as a threat, but simply a consequence you will need to administer in order to protect yourself against what you perceive to be a threat. Your enemy may choose to remove the threat in order to keep his or her own power and free will. Whenever you impose your will on another person, expect to escalate the animosity between the two of you, so again consider binding to be a last resort.

A binding is best performed during a waning moon on a Saturday, since the declining moon energies can help your enemy's harmful energies to fade, and Saturday is associated with endings and destruction. If you choose, you can perform your binding within a magic circle, so refer to the section on how to cast a magic circle if you don't know how to do that already. You will need either a photograph of your enemy or a small doll that can represent your enemy; wax is the traditional material. You will also need a long black cord, string, or ribbon, and a place to store the charm you make, preferably a locking box.

If you choose to cast a circle, do so first with all of your supplies inside. Prepare a photograph, if you have one, by cutting out your enemy if there is anyone else in the photo. Make sure that you do not bind any other people in the picture. If you choose to use a wax figure or other doll, you can add features to remind you of your enemy. If you have access to any objects used by your enemy, you can include those, but please don't steal any objects from your enemy. For example, if you are binding your child, you can dress the doll in old, outgrown clothes that were marked for discarding or donation. You can also put in the doll's hand a discarded piece of paper the person used and then tossed in the wastebasket. Traditionally, hair left on a brush has been used. Close your eyes and visualize your enemy completely bound with rope and rendered harmless to you or anyone else.

If you are using a photograph, begin by tying a loop of the cord tightly around the picture's middle and securing it with a knot. Wrap the cord tightly around the object counterclockwise if you are looking down at the head of your enemy from the top and wrapping around the middle. If you are using a wax figure or other doll, secure the hands first behind the back like handcuffs and wrap half the cord tightly. Bring the feet of the figure behind the doll so that it is kneeling and wrap the feet without cutting the cord. As you wrap, you can chant the following:

> *As I speak this charm*
> *As this cord I wind*
> *No hex can harm*
> *Your danger I bind.*

When you are done, knot a final loop to secure the cord to your ritual object. Ground the energy that you have built thoroughly and take down any magic circle that you set up. Store the object in a locked box somewhere where nobody will find it. Some people choose to bury the object, since a binding is meant to be a permanent ritual. In fact, I highly recommend holding off on a binding if you feel even slightly like you might want to reverse it. However, if you do change your mind, you can attempt to reverse a binding by cutting the cords carefully away from the object while chanting:

> *Blessed be*
> *You are free*
> *With harm to none*
> *So mote it be!*

Afterward, the freed photograph or figure should be burned. However, be ready for a binding reversal to have the potential not to work at all. Some people's energy seems to conform to containment, and if there is to be any healing to the point where they can defend themselves again, it may be slow to develop and not as effective as before. Again, only use a binding if you feel certain that you will not change your mind.

CUTTING CORDS

Cutting a cord is another ritual designed to be permanent and create a separation between you and your enemy forever. Cutting a cord is not well suited, for this reason, to family members with whom you will have to interact in the future, or to someone else on whom you will depend for partnership now or in the future, like an ex who shares child custody, or a boss at work. However, cutting a cord is well suited to an abusive ex-partner when no child custody issues are involved. Be advised that cutting the cord will not instantly make you stop missing him or her, but it will remove the energetic ties through which hexes can most easily operate.

Cutting the cord takes some mundane planning at first. Begin by clearing your home, office, car, or any other space that reminds you of your enemy. Contrary to cultural myth, the objects belonging to your enemy that you possess don't have to be burned, but if they are yours and are safe to burn, you may do so if it helps you release the memories and emotions associated with them. You can donate the objects or simply throw them away, but don't store them. Delete your enemy's phone number and other contact information from all your electronics in addition to any electronic correspondence or connections with him or her. Clear all photos and postings, for instance, relating to the person from your social networking sites.

If you have any photographs of the two of you together, they can be used in the ritual if you like. You will need a sharp pair of scissors or a ritual knife either way. Cutting the cord is best done during a waning moon on a Saturday, just like a binding ritual. Begin by casting a magic circle if you wish. If you have photographs of the two of you together, cut them apart so that the two of you are separated. Then close your eyes and visualize a cord that comes from your solar plexus, like an umbilical cord from your belly button, extending out into the universe and across whatever distance to your intended. Take up your ritual knife or the sharp pair of scissors, and cut this cord away from your body, about arm's length from your belly button. Visualize the cord disintegrating as it is destroyed. You can speak the following charm three times:

> *I cut the cord*
> *I sever ties*
> *We harm none,*
> *Live separate lives.*

When you are done, thoroughly ground the energy you have raised. You may burn the cut photographs either inside your circle if you have created one, or within the next twenty-four hours if it is impractical to destroy them right away. Take down your magic circle, and discard the ashes from any burned photographs in running water, or you can bury them. A ritual to cut ties with another is permanent, so it will be very difficult for you if you change your mind. Rather than doing another ritual to tie the two of you together, you'd best try the normal way of starting from scratch and building a brand new relationship together, but be aware that you'd be fighting upstream through your own magic and your past choices.

Conclusion

It is my deepest hope that this book has given you the strength to fight bad luck and hexes, wherever you go in life. Maybe you're disappointed—or maybe you're relieved. You now have information about genuine hexes and the mind games that your brain can play that look a lot like hexes. You're equipped with multiple weapons against the evils of human nature, both inside you and out in the world.

As you move forward, past whatever incidents may have prompted you to study this subject, keep your critical thinking and insight close at hand. Trust your own intuition to divine the source of your bad luck, hex, or simple misunderstanding. Get to the bottom of problems rather than ignoring them or living in fear.

Whether or not you've been the victim of a hex, take stock of the hex prevention strategies and tools at your disposal, and decide what measures you should take right away that fit your lifestyle. Everyone can afford to prevent feuds by treating people from other cultures or fellow magical practitioners with compassion and understanding. I personally believe that everyone should undertake psychic hygiene practices like grounding, aura cleansing, shielding, and prayer as serious disciplines. However, don't overwhelm yourself with a huge list of homework to perform every morning under the fear that a hex will befall you if you don't do the work. Start with becoming mindful of grounding, cleansing, shielding, and prayer, and you'll beef up your natural magical immune system enough to withstand a hex more readily than when you are at your most vulnerable. Only once you've mastered the basics should you start thinking about becoming proficient with other ritual techniques that can help form you into an advanced defensive practitioner of magic.

Look deeper within yourself and psychoanalyze your habits of mind and the ways you react when you encounter negative events or people in your life. There may be some steps you can take for your body, mind, and soul that can make you a healthier person and ensure that thoughts of a hex don't need to tiptoe across your mind any time something in your life goes awry. Most of all, make sure that you are not inadvertently hexing yourself or others with your thoughts. You may find yourself turning into your own worst enemy if you are not careful in keeping control of your internal dialogue and the actions that result. Reach out to a counselor or to other resources if serious issues from your past or from your way of thinking hamper your everyday enjoyment of life, ability to work, or ability to form healthy relationships with others.

Acquaint yourself thoroughly with hex removal techniques, but try not to obsess over fantasies of removing your own hexes if you've found that you're unlikely to encounter them at all. You needn't make yourself jumpy with the hasty desire to perform a hex removal at the first sign of danger. Instead, try to focus your energy outward into your community and offer to help anyone who may think a hex or curse is plaguing them. By donating your energy to others, even those who might be enemies, you contribute to making the world a better place. For every hex you remove or curse caster you soothe, you eliminate more malicious magic from the world and make it safer for you and the people you care about.

Quell any ill feelings about your enemies, and consider giving this book as a gift to those who hex, those who think they have been hexed, or to your neighborhood psychic practitioner as a way to reach out and eliminate black magic in your corner of the world. Remember, a thief in your neighborhood may be the result of a neighbor and potential friend in wanting. Likewise, if there is a curse caster near you, be assured that such a person is suffering and radiating pain to those around him or her. Give of yourself freely in order to alleviate suffering in your immediate surroundings, and your kindness will radiate outward to the rest of the globe through the magical laws of energy. Those who sow seeds of change spin the wheel of rebirth. Be an instrument of change and rebirth whenever you feel constrained by fear, and you will find a power inside of you that you may not even have known was there.

Glossary

Ablution: Washing oneself for the purpose of spiritual purification.

Amulet: An object, usually from nature, worn or carried on a person to ward off danger or to perform some other spell purpose.

Aura: A halo of energy that surrounds all living things. Auras can be perceived by some people visually, or in the mind's eye, or through other sensory perception or use of a pendulum.

Banishing: A ritual performed with the purpose to rid a place of malevolent entities or energy.

Black Magic: Malicious magic performed with the goal to produce negative effects on a target.

Cleansing: A spiritual ritual performed to rid a person, place, or object of malevolent energy.

Demon: A catch-all term for a malevolent entity. Some religious faith traditions believe demons to have only evil motives.

Divination: The use of tools or a system of understanding in order to discover true answers about the past, present, and future.

Elemental: A natural entity associated with an element of earth, air, fire, or water that can be mischievous.

Energy: Unlike the scientific definition of energy, in the context of this book energy refers to the life force or *chi* that flows through the universe and through living things. Energy is used to create and to break hexes.

Exorcism: A ritual performed with the purpose to remove the presence of a malevolent entity from an object or person.

Fetter: An object used to house an elemental, ghost, or malevolent entity, usually against its will.

Ghost: The spirit of a person who has died that remains in some form on earth. It can be malevolent or harmless.

Grounding: The practice of pushing stuck or excess energy out of the body into the earth and drawing fresh energy back into the body in order to produce an alert but calm state of being.

Karma: A natural spiritual law that dictates that positive actions or magic can bring positive energetic results back to the practitioner, while negative magic or actions can have a bad effect on the practitioner, in this life or the next.

Law of Association: If two or more things have commonalities, they can be used in magic together in order to associate ideas with each other.

Law of Contagion: Objects that are in contact with one another—physically or spiritually—will continue to be connected through magic even when they are separated.

Law of Knowledge: The more you know about something or someone, the more able you will be to control it through magic.

Law of Names: Knowing the full, real name of a person can be used in magic to gain influence over that person.

Law of Negative Attraction: Opposites can attract each other, and this concept is used in magic to create a balance between objects or concepts used in a ritual.

Law of Positive Attraction: Like can attract like, so when practicing magic, a person may put out the kind of energy into the universe that they wish to bring back to themselves. *See also* karma.

Law of Similarity: In magic, creating a lookalike target or effect upon a target can aid the real outcome upon the actual target of the working.

Law of Synchronicity: True coincidences are rare, so if two things happen at the same time, they are likely to be magically associated.

Magic: The act of changing one's world in accordance with will using the mind, energy, and potentially other spiritual sources.

Pendulum: A weight suspended from a string that is allowed to swing freely from a person's hand. The pendulum does not move on its own, but is used as an indicator of the person's subconscious movements to amplify psychic answers.

Psychic: The use of senses other than the ordinary five in order to discover past, present, or future truths.

Psychic Vampire: A human who drains spiritual energy from another person (purposely or unconsciously), often without consent.

Sigil: A magical symbol used to represent a concept, person, place, group, or thing.

Spirit: A term that can mean the source of divinity, or a magical entity such as a ghost, demon, or elemental.

Talisman: A charm that is created to be worn or carried by a person for a specific purpose, usually protection.

Tarot: A deck of seventy-eight cards used in divination.

Zaar: A dance used for healing or exorcism purposes.

Bibliography

Byrne, Rhonda. *The Secret.* New York: Atria Books, 2006.

Crème, Benjamin. *Transmission: A Meditation for the New Age.* London: Share International, 1983.

Cunningham, Scott. *Divination for Beginners.* Woodbury, MN: Llewellyn Publications, 2003.

Dyer, Wayne W. *There's a Spiritual Solution to Every Problem.* New York: HarperCollins, 2001.

Eddy, Mary Baker. *Science and Health with Key to the Scriptures.* Boston: Christian Science Board of Directors, 1875.

Foster, Richard J. *Prayer—10th Anniversary Edition: Finding the Heart's True Home.* New York: HarperCollins, 1992.

Gile, Robin, and Lisa Lenard. *The Complete Idiot's Guide to Palmistry.* Indianapolis: Amaranth, 1999.

Greenwood, Carmel. *Letting Go and Loving Life.* London: Rider and Co., 2000.

Meyer, Joyce. *Approval Addiction: Overcoming Your Need to Please Everyone.* New York: Time Warner Book Group, 2005.

Penczak, Christopher. *The Witch's Shield: Protection Magick and Psychic Self-Defense.* Woodbury, MN: Llewellyn Publications, 2008.

Starhawk. *The Spiral Dance: A Rebirth of the Ancient Religion of the Great Goddess.* New York: HarperOne, 1989.

Tolle, Eckhart. *The Power of Now: A Guide to Spiritual Enlightenment.* Novato, CA: New World Library, 1999.